The Great MOONPIE® HANDBOOK

The Great MOONPIE® HANDBOOK

By
Ron Dickson

(With help from William M. Clark, Marion Hankins,
Linda Whitener, Paul Seid, Paul Shelley, and Ralph Grigg)

Illustrated
by Sam C. Rawls

PELICAN PUBLISHING
NEW ORLEANS

Copyright © 1985, 2010
By Ron Dickson

Illustrations copyright © 1985, 2010
By Sam C. Rawls
All rights reserved

First published by Peachtree Publishers, Ltd., 1985
Published by arrangement with the author by
    Pelican Publishing Company, Inc., 2010

First edition, 1985
First Pelican edition, 2010
Second printing, 2023

*The word "Pelican" and the depiction of a pelican
are trademarks of Arcadia Publishing Company Inc.
and are registered in the U.S. Patent and Trademark Office.*

Library of Congress Cataloging-in-Publication Data

Dickson, Ron.
  The great Moonpie handbook / by Ron Dickson ; with help from William M. Clark ... [et al.] ; illustrated by Sam C. Rawls. -- 1st Pelican ed.
      p. cm.
  On t.p. the registered trademark symbol "R" appears after "moonpie."
  Originally published as: The great American moon pie handbook. Atlanta, Ga. : Peachtree Publishers, 1985.
    ISBN 978-1-58980-857-7 (pbk. : alk. paper) 1. Moon Pies--Humor. I. Clark, William M., 1948- II. Rawls, Sam C. III. Dickson, Ron. Great American moon pie handbook. IV. Title.
  PN6231.M672D5 2010
  818'.5402--dc22
                                    2010027667

"Moon Pie®" and "MoonPie®" are registered in the U.S. Patent and Trademark Office by the Chattanooga Bakery, Inc., for its brand of marshmallow sandwich. The words must be capitalized.

Printed in the United States of America
Published by Pelican Publishing
New Orleans, LA
www.pelicanpub.com

To Elizabeth Anne Dickson (environmental analyst, Vermont), Cynthia Jean Dickson Lindberg (architect, New York City), Sarah Elizabeth Lindberg (student, Brooklyn), John W. "Will" Dickson (landscape designer, Charlotte), Lynda Stinson Hollar (North Carolina), and Elisabeth Søyland (dermatologist, Oslo), who have all generously supported my dedication to the handbook and the Noble Cause.

Special thanks are due Jeanne Bridges, whose love and devotion encouraged me to prepare the Pelican edition, and Jean A. Chase, whose friendship and support motivated me to continue seeking a publisher. —Ronald W. Dickson

To Janet, whose cheerful encouragement made this project a delightful experience. —Sam C. Rawls ("SCRAWLS")

To my parents, William and Dorothy, who constantly encouraged me to finish school and move out as quickly as possible.
—William M. Clark

Disclaimer

This book was prepared with information believed to be accurate but without the direct participation of the Chattanooga Bakery, Inc. Neither the president, sales manager, manager of distribution, master baker, nor any other Bakery employee can be held liable for any errors or omissions.

All statements of fact in this book are either accurate or otherwise.

The original name of the product was Moon®Pie, with the registered trademark symbol between the two words. In 1996, the symbol was moved after the words: MoonPie®.

Throughout this book, the author uses the name "MoonPie." The "®" symbol has been omitted in the text for clarity.

Cheerwine®, Oreo®, and Fig Newton® are other trademarks mentioned in the text.

Contents

	Acknowledgments	11
Chapter 1	In the Beginning	17
Chapter 2	Spreading the Word	35
Chapter 3	MoonPie Madness	45
Chapter 4	Savoring the Noble Snack	56
Chapter 5	The Sensuous Woman and MoonPies	71
Chapter 6	The MoonPie Effect	78
Chapter 7	Childrearing—The MoonPie Method	89
Chapter 8	MoonPie Over My Hammy	94
Chapter 9	Entertaining MoonPie Style	99
Chapter 10	MoonPie-in-the-Sky Plans	107
Chapter 11	The Impact of MoonPies Upon the World	134
Chapter 12	The Man in the Moon	143
Chapter 13	The MoonPie Tradition	149
	Appendix	152

Acknowledgments

Anna P. Pratt, granddaughter of the inventor of the MoonPie, Earl W. Mitchell, provided the author with several photographs and stories about Mr. Mitchell and his family. Anna worked as an editor for the federal government. She revised the text of this book, thus making many improvements. Her support and encouragement for several years inspired the author to continue working on the manuscript.

The entire staff of the Chattanooga Bakery, Inc., has been most helpful and encouraging with the creation of this book.

For the second edition, special thanks are due to the following people.

Sam Campbell IV, President, continues to encourage my efforts as the official Goodwill Ambassador for the MoonPie (entirely without monetary compensation). For many, many years he has supplied me with free samples of MoonPies. Being on Sam's "comp list" is a greater honor than the Nobel Peace Prize or the Pulitzer Prize. Those prizes are just money moldering in musty bank vaults. My honor

Courtesy of John Campbell

has enabled me to bring delight to thousands of fans and joy to those deprived souls who had never enjoyed the noble snack.

Courtesy of John Campbell

John Campbell, Vice President, supplied me with hats, T-shirts, and polo shirts that I proudly wore from North Carolina to Florida, California, Vermont, Hawaii, Canada, and Norway.

Courtesy of John Campbell

Tory Johnston, Director of Marketing, inspired me with his fresh ideas.

Courtesy of John Campbell

Guy Callahan, Operations, kept all the units of the Bakery working together harmoniously.

Courtesy of John Campbell

Matt Fuller, Shipping Department Manager, promptly sent me samples of the MoonPie for many years, bringing joy into the lives of thousands of people.

Courtesy of John Campbell

Keith Holt, Controller, kept an honest set of books, thus depriving himself of ever getting an appointment in the federal government.

Courtesy of John Campbell

The ladies of the support staff, Fredia Higdon, Fran Reid, Linda Shell, Beverly Sanders, Linda Fowlkes, and Janice McFarland (left to right), cheerfully tracked down people at the Bakery for me. Their courteous, friendly manner always implied that the sun was shining brightly in Chattanooga.

And finally, Bill Clark, previously of New York State, enthusiastically contributed several clever and profound stories. Needing a sense of direction and noble purpose in his life, he also became the first editor of this handbook. He rescued many ideas expressed in a crude manner and rewrote them in a polished form. His enthusiasm kept the project moving ahead.

The Great MOONPIE® HANDBOOK

CHAPTER 1

In the Beginning

In 1917 the sun shined brightly on Chattanooga, Tennessee, and the MoonPie was brought forth upon this land. In the decades since that fateful day, people of exceptional breeding and strong appetite have been nurtured by this heavenly delight. People living in unfortunate cultures (usually places covered with snow and ice) have asked Southerners, "Jeez, guys, what da heck's a MoonPie?"

Connoisseurs of the noble snack take great pride in answering that question. A regular MoonPie consists of two cookies, each about four inches in diameter and reminiscent of graham crackers, although the exact recipe is a closely guarded secret. Between the two cookies is a layer of marshmallow approximately one-quarter inch thick. Depending upon the flavor to be created, the sandwich is drenched with a generous quantity of chocolate, vanilla, banana, lemon, orange, or strawberry flavored coating. The result is a delicious pastry with just enough moisture to produce a wonderful snack food. The original MoonPie was approximately four and a half inches in diameter and sold for a nickel. If it tasted any better, it would probably be illegal.

The Chattanooga Bakery, Inc., was founded in the early 1900s as a subsidiary of the Mountain City Flour Mill in Chattanooga, Tennessee. The Bakery's original purpose was to use the excess flour produced by the mill. By 1910, the Bakery offered over two hundred different confectionery items. In 1917, it developed a product that is still known as the MoonPie.

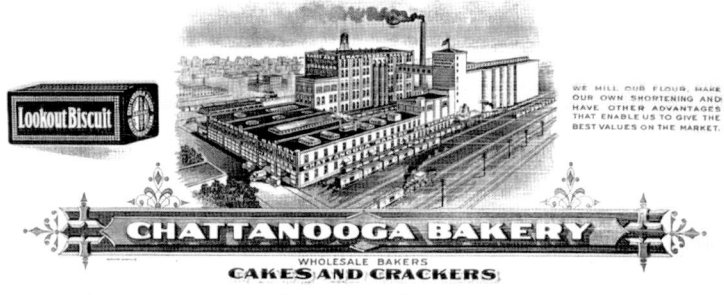

Ancient letterhead of the Chattanooga Bakery

Marketing history was made in 1969 when the Chattanooga Bakery introduced the Double Decker MoonPie, featuring two layers of marshmallow and three delectable cookies. John Kosik, later the executive vice president, suggested the idea to other managers at the Bakery around 1968. He listened to customers' requests for a bigger MoonPie but realized that vending machines couldn't accept a larger diameter. His idea was to "go up" by adding another layer of marshmallow and another cookie. He took his idea to Jim Sanders, the Bakery's engineer, and a test run was arranged.

John Kosik (circa 1968)

Six cookies came down the conveyer belt and marshmallow was squirted on them. Then cookies were placed on top of the marshmallow on three pies, leaving three items that were then turned over and put onto the original three pies. This made a double decker in small quantities suitable for the test. The double deckers were so good that production began in earnest shortly thereafter. The double decker first sold for fifteen cents in convenience stores.

The Mini MoonPie was introduced in 1998, and the Fruit Filled MoonPie (at first called the Full Moon) was introduced in 2001 but discontinued in 2004.

The modern MoonPie closely resembles the original in size and composition, an excellent example of a quality product surviving the advance of "progress." This is indeed a rarity in this age of artificial ingredients. Unlike the makers of other snack foods, who have reduced both the size and quality of their products over the years, the Bakery has maintained the high quality of its original marshmallow sandwich. Its motto is, "If it ain't broke, don't fix it."

Allegedly, someone at the Bakery in 1984 gave this advice to the Coca-Cola Company in Atlanta when they were beginning to advertise the "New Coke." Coca-Cola, however, proceeded with their plans and created a disaster. Perhaps that inspired the following cartoon.

Cartoon by Clyde Wells, Augusta Chronicle

The famed marshmallow sandwich has an unusually long shelf life of about four months.

For over seventy-five years, MoonPie sandwiches were wrapped in clear cellophane so that the distinctive colors showed through. This enabled customers to pick up the flavor of their choice. The banana MoonPie is a delicate yellow color; vanilla is creamy white; chocolate is dark brown; strawberry is light pink; and lemon is pale yellow. Consequently, even illiterate customers were assured of getting the MoonPie of their choice. Color-blind illiterate customers had to seek assistance from sympathetic clerks.

Around the turn of the century (2000), the Bakery began using colored cellophane wrappers to make the packaging more vivid. The chocolate wrapper is a bright blue to make this most popular flavor stand out. The wrappers for other flavors are also colored to match the contents.

No records have been kept on the total number of Moon-Pies sold since 1917, and current sales and production figures are confidential. Some fans estimate that the Bakery produces several hundred thousand MoonPies a day. This chart shows current packaging options for the MoonPie.

MoonPie Packaging Options

Product	Flavors	Packaging
Original Single Decker	Vanilla, Banana, and Chocolate	Cases of 8 boxes with 12 pies and 50-count vending-machine boxes
Double Decker	Vanilla, Banana, and Chocolate	Cases of 6 boxes with 12 pies, cases of 8 boxes with 8 pies, cases of 16 boxes with 4 pies, and 48-count vending-machine boxes
Double Decker	Lemon, Orange, and Strawberry	Cases of 6 boxes with 12 pies and 48-count vending-machine boxes
Mini	Vanilla, Banana, Orange, and Chocolate	Cases of 12 boxes with 12 pies; chocolate also comes in cases of 12 boxes with 8 pies and 150-count vending-machine boxes

The popularity of the MoonPie isn't limited to the United States. In the 1980s, the Chattanooga Bakery entered into a licensing agreement with the Tohato Baking Company of Japan to produce "Massi Pies." "Massi" means marshmallow in Japanese and is used instead of the word "Moon," since that word is sacred in Japan.

The success of the original marshmallow sandwich has attracted numerous imitators, but none can use the name

"MoonPie" because it is trademarked. Lowly imitations must have their own name or use the term "marshmallow sandwich." While it would be discourteous to mention names, it should be noted that one of the imitators has achieved incredible success in duplicating exactly the flavor and texture of cardboard, another has perfectly reproduced the texture and aroma of sawdust, and yet another has matched the texture of glue. These pretenders, miffed by their inability to unseat the King of Pies, have conducted campaigns of rumor and innuendo against MoonPies for years without success.

The Chattanooga Bakery celebrated 100 years of success in 2003. The following chart lists some milestones in its history.

Chattanooga Bakery Milestones

1903	The Chattanooga Bakery, Inc., is established.
1917	The MoonPie is created.
1969	The Double Decker MoonPie, featuring two layers of marshmallow and three delectable cookies, is introduced.
1985	The Bakery moves from its original building to a larger facility on Manufacturers Road in Chattanooga.
1996	The American Dairy Council features MoonPies on billboards across the land with its "Got Milk?" slogan. The trademark is changed from "Moon®Pie" to "MoonPie®."
1998	The Mini MoonPie is introduced.
1998/1999	The Bakery becomes a marketing partner with NASCAR. The MoonPie is designated the "Official Snack Cake of NASCAR."
2001	The Full Moon (later called the Fruit Filled MoonPie) is introduced.
2004	Several new flavors are introduced, such as lemon, orange, and strawberry. The Bakery continues to produce its old favorites—chocolate, vanilla, and banana. The Full Moon is discontinued.
2009	Mini Peanut Butter MoonPie and Mint Crunch MoonPie are introduced.

MoonPie Logos Through the Years

The original logo had only yellow ink for the moon. Sometimes the moon was not very noticeable, especially on T-shirts and other garments. Around 1985, a member of the MoonPie Cultural Club suggested to the Bakery that the moon would be more distinct if it were outlined with blue ink. According to John Kosik, then executive vice president, the Bakery's advertising agency was already considering a similar idea. In the mid- to late 1980s, the moon was indeed outlined with blue ink.

The Delta MoonPie was a small, double decker marshmallow sandwich

In 2009, the Mini MoonPie had a smiling face for the "man in the moon"

The Lookout pie is a single decker

The Mint Crunch box has this logo

The Peanut Butter Crunch box has this design

Universal Appeal

From being a snack with only limited regional appeal, the fame of the MoonPie has spread around the world. Foreign visitors to the South have enjoyed the MoonPie, and many have sent packages of the snacks back to their homelands. In one instance, some overseas visitors returning home ordered enough MoonPies to fill an air cargo container. Foreigners living in the U.S. are some of the MoonPie's most dedicated and enthusiastic fans. The MoonPie can now be found almost anywhere—its appeal is truly universal.

After the first edition of this book was published in 1985, it became socially acceptable to share MoonPies with cultured and refined friends from all backgrounds. The snack was no longer considered something fit only for Southern rednecks, millworkers, farmhands, and other members of the working class. The snack also started getting mentioned in newspaper articles, discussed on National Public Radio, and featured on television programs. In 1989, the MoonPie earned a place in the prestigious *Encyclopedia of Southern Culture* (The University of North Carolina Press, page 696).

Within a few weeks of the first printing of this handbook, people sighted MoonPie T-shirts in a prestigious office in Manhattan; on the shores of a famous resort lake in New Hampshire; in Tampa, Florida; in Boogertown, North Carolina (a suburb of Gastonia); and at The School of Design (architecture) at North Carolina State University in Raleigh. Around 1990, the American Folk Art Museum in New York City had an exhibition of Southern folk art. For the prestigious opening, a chef cut MoonPies into quarters and served them on silver platters to ladies and gentlemen in formal evening wear. These sophisticated people believed that the chef had labored for many hours to prepare these delicious treats and never realized that they were MoonPies. (This was reported by Cynthia D. Lindberg.)

Inventor of the MoonPie Discovered by the Author

The first edition of this book was published on April 1, 1985, a date carefully selected to emphasize the scholarly nature of the work.

Shortly after, the *New York Times* published a story about the book and the MoonPie. This article was reprinted in a newspaper in Columbia, South Carolina. Earl Wayne Mitchell, Jr., read the story about the forgotten origin of the MoonPie and called the *New York Times* to get the telephone number of Ron Dickson, the author of the handbook. Mr. Mitchell explained to Ron that his daddy, Earl Sr., had invented the MoonPie around 1917 or 1918. He told how he had accompanied his daddy on his rounds as a traveling salesman for the Chattanooga Bakery. He often drove the car for his weary dad.

Mr. Mitchell's story goes like this. Early in the 1900s, while servicing his territory of Kentucky, Tennessee, and

West Virginia, Mr. Mitchell was visiting a company store that catered to the coal miners. He asked them what they might enjoy as a snack. The miners said they wanted something for their lunch pails. It had to be solid and filling. "About how big?" Mr. Mitchell asked.

Well, about that time the moon was rising, so a miner held out his big hands, framing the moon, and said, "About that big!"

Upon Mr. Mitchell's return to the Bakery, he noticed some of the workers dipping one side of graham cookies into marshmallow and laying them on the windowsill to harden until lunchtime. Mr. Mitchell had a sudden, brilliant inspiration. He put another cookie on top for a lid and took a bunch of them to the coal miners. They tried his creation but said it needed something like chocolate frosting to be a tasty snack.

Back at the Bakery, Mr. Mitchell added a generous coating of chocolate and took them back for the workers to try. In fact, the Bakery also sent MoonPie samples around with its other salespeople. The response was so overwhelmingly positive that the MoonPie became a regular item for the Bakery. Thus, the world was changed forevermore.

Ron Dickson, ever skeptical of someone trying to pull his leg, asked the younger Mr. Mitchell one question to verify the story about his father. "How did the Bakery get flour delivered? Was it by truck, train, wagon, or some other means?"

Without a second's hesitation, Mr. Mitchell said, "The flour mill was behind the rear wall of the Bakery. When the Bakery needed flour, a man pulled up a sliding trap door in the back wall and flour poured down a chute into a buggy bigger than a bathtub." Only if Mr. Mitchell had been in the Bakery would he know about the delivery of flour.

When Dickson had toured the Bakery, he had inquired about the big chute and the trap door. How many casual visitors would ask about the purpose of the chute? Not many. Dickson's friends consider him to be a very curious fellow, or should we say, politely, "a fellow with a great sense of curiosity"?

Realizing that he had solved the mystery of the creation

of the MoonPie, Ron drove to Mr. Mitchell's house in Columbia, South Carolina for an interview and photography session. Mr. Mitchell had old letters from the Chattanooga Milling Company addressed to his father and photographs of his father.

When Ron returned to Charlotte, he alerted the *Charlotte Observer* about the scoop of the century. That afternoon, the *Observer* sent a reporter and photographer to interview Mr. Mitchell. The story was printed on the front page of the *Observer*.

Cosmic Coincidence?

Earl *Wayne* Mitchell invented the MoonPie in 1917. When a son was born to Brady Wilson Dickson and his wife, Isabel Davis Dickson, in Shelby, North Carolina on November 11, 1932, they wondered what to name him. In a sudden burst of inspiration, the father suggested Ronald *Wayne* Dickson.

Was it just a coincidence that the creator of the MoonPie and this infant had the same middle name? Was it destiny that this little boy would later write about the MoonPie? Was it fate that he would passionately devote his life (at least his spare time) to spreading the good news about the MoonPie and the benefits of humor in life? Was it mental telepathy? Was it a coincidence that the father had enjoyed a MoonPie and a soft drink in the afternoon before that romantic evening some nine months and six hours before Ronald *Wayne* was born? If Mr. Dickson had enjoyed two MoonPies, would he have come up with the other given name of Mr. Mitchell, "*Earl*"? It leads one to ponder deep philosophical and cosmological possibilities (whatever *they* are).

Monument to the Unknown Salesman

MoonPie fans debated for years about the best way to honor the genius who suggested the design of the original pie, even though his identity was unknown at the time. At a meeting of the MoonPie Cultural Club in Chattanooga, students, housewives, doctors, engineers, and historians—in short, a true cross section of America—crafted what has since come to be known among devotees as the Chattanooga Proclamation. Briefly, the Chattanooga Proclamation stated that "artists, craftsmen, architects and school children from around the world shall be invited to submit designs, drawings, and scale models of a proposed monument depicting the unknown salesman and his invention." At the conclusion of the meeting, a subcommittee was formed to begin distribution of the official invitations to all chapters. The response from around the world was overwhelming and showed brilliant bursts of creativity. The author feels that it is important to print a few of the best ideas to demonstrate the passionate replies.

The Lookout Mountain Proposal

This proposed carving in stone on the side of Lookout Mountain, not far from Chattanooga, would rival that of the presidents on Mount Rushmore and the Civil War heroes on Stone Mountain near Atlanta, Georgia. The design is of a traveling salesman handing a MoonPie to a small child. This proposal could be modified to include rows of adults in the background weeping with joy.

The Pooveyville Proposal

Submitted by a swimming pool contractor from Pooveyville, Georgia, the design called for the construction of a giant concrete shoe. "The shoe would be approximately forty feet long and twenty feet wide and would symbolize the traveling salesman's most essential piece of equipment," the designer wrote. "It would be built out of reinforced concrete and have the finest quality plastic liner available to the industry. During the summer months it could be used for swimming and diving, while in the winter it would be a reflecting pool. As to the type of shoe,

The sculpture on Lookout Mountain

I would suggest a saddle shoe, although an oxford or a wing tip would not be beyond reason." The Pooveyville Proposal concluded with the designer's suggestion that "for a small nominal fee I could provide a custom canvas cover shaped like a spat." The proposal, of course, remains under consideration.

The Heidelberg Design

Surprisingly, one of the most interesting designs came from the Heidelberg Institute of Kinetic Art. Submitted by a group of graduate students, this design called for a stainless steel suitcase perched upon a stainless steel pedestal. The hydraulically operated suitcase would open to reveal four stainless steel MoonPies revolving around a blinking lightbulb. While the symbolism of the individual components is clear, what is unclear is the actual size of the sculpture. The designers' statement that "it should be very large to convey the significance of the historic event, but small enough not to impede low level aircraft" leaves room for considerable speculation.

The Marcia Mooney Letter

The MoonPie Cultural Club received the following letter from a Miss Marcia Mooney of Johnson City, Kansas:

> Dear Mr. MoonPie People:
> I love MoonPies. My mother gives them to me every day for dessert. I would like to tell you how the Unknown Salesman statue should be. First you take two hundred MoonPies and you put them on top of each other for legs. Then you take fifty MoonPies for arms. Next get the MoonPie factory to make a special big MoonPie for the head. Two vanilla MoonPies could be eyes. This would be the salesman.
> Your friend,
> Marcia
> P.S. Could you please send me one of those special big MoonPies for a prize?

The New York School of Modern Art Design

The proposed monument should be in the form of a "Plexiglas bowler or derby representing the attire of an early twentieth century salesman," came the recommendation from the cultural hub of the United States. "Inside the bowler would be a cube painted with the four basic steps in the preparation of MoonPies." Unfortunately, several members of the Cultural Club objected to this design on the basis that the essence of something as exotically delicious as the MoonPie cannot be reduced to four simple steps.

The Hinkley, Ohio, Proposal

From Hinkley, Ohio, whose only claim to fame is the return each spring of the buzzards, came the following suggestion:

It should be, of course, a large marble statue in the tradition of all public monuments. The statue should clearly represent a salesman with one hand extended (as if poised for a handshake) and with a briefcase in the other hand. The only feature that would clearly distinguish this as being The Unknown Salesman is the complete lack of a face.
—William M. Clark

The Cultural Club's reaction was that Hinkley should stick with the buzzards.

The Hinkley, Ohio, design

The Flagstaff Design

The School of Design of the University of Arizona at Flagstaff is among the leaders in new concepts of solar energy, and the Flagstaff Design, suggested by Ralph W. Grigg, Esq., reflected this specialization. It called for a huge solar dome made of clear glass or plastic with the MoonPie logo painted upon it, the overall appearance being that of a MoonPie wrapper slightly inflated. Inside would be a gigantic MoonPie carved out of stone with a natural chocolate color. This would be a solar heat collector. On top of the MoonPie would be a statue of the unknown salesman in a standing position, apparently talking to someone. He would hold a MoonPie gently in his right hand, and his sample case would rest at his feet. The solar heat collected by this memorial would be conducted a short distance to the Home for Retired Traveling Salesmen. It should be noted that this design repelled pigeons.

The Flagstaff Design had the twin benefits of being attractive and providing heat to the home, thus paying for the cost of the monument. Vegetables could also be grown inside the dome.

The University of Melbourne (Australia) Design

This design called for a large structure in the shape of a MoonPie box with the lid raised in the display position (with the lid folded in half and then placed upright). The stained glass skylights, when seen from above, would look like MoonPie wrappers.

Inside would be a bronze statue of the mythical, unknown salesman. Of course, he would be holding a MoonPie in one hand and a soft drink in the other. The walls of the edifice would be adorned with pictures showing historic events about the Bakery and the MoonPie. These pictures would be obtained from the Chattanooga Museum of Fine Arts.

In the outer walls would be huge stained glass windows with the following scenes: pictures of all flavors and sizes of MoonPies, portraits of the founders of the Bakery, and portraits of twelve famous traveling salesmen who first sold MoonPies to the far ends of the continent. A profusion of live green plants would add to the decor.

The center of the structure would contain a huge sidewalk cafe serving all flavors of MoonPies and carefully selected beverages. Thus, pilgrims could rest their feet, refresh their bodies, and enjoy the significance of the memorial.

Go West Young Man, for a MoonPie

Several years ago, any MoonPie connoisseur traveling to the West Coast had to fend for him- or herself. That region of the country was so depraved that few people even knew of MoonPies. The mere mention of the noble snack would evoke such responses as: "Omigod! MoonPies? Barf me out! Isn't that, ya know, like when some dude cruises like, ya know, Sunset Boulevard and sticks his butt out the window of a Mercedes? Sooo grody! Like, to the max!"

Or, "MoonPie? Yeah, man, I know her. Zappa's daughter."

Or, "MoonPies? Aren't those the bald guys in bed sheets who sell flowers at the airport?"

In a humanitarian attempt to introduce California to the Age of Enlightenment, the Chattanooga Bakery at last opened a West Coast distribution center. We are all most grateful, like, to the max!

CHAPTER 2

Spreading the Word

When this book was first published, the Bakery, realizing its promotional value, sent boxes of Double Decker Chocolate MoonPies and copies of the book to 250 book reviewers. Newspapers around the country soon started printing stories about the MoonPie. The publisher and the Bakery learned an important lesson—newspaper people are always looking for new story ideas (and they appreciate free food).

The growing appeal of MoonPies was documented in 1984 when Doug Marlette, award-winning editorial cartoonist for the *Charlotte Observer* and creator of the nationally syndicated comic strip "Kudzu," devoted two weeks of his popular strip to the noble snack.

Marlette, who says that an early draft of this book inspired him, was duly recognized and honored by the MoonPie Cultural Club as the very first "Champion of the MoonPie." For his contribution to MoonPie lore, the club presented Marlette with a gourmet selection of pies, an official T-shirt and cap, and an official MoonPie embroidered emblem, suitable for sewing onto his favorite jacket.

Other cartoonists also featured the MoonPie in their work. During a rare blizzard in March 1993, the *Charlotte Observer* featured a cartoon by Kevin Siers showing a Saint Bernard bringing RC Colas® and MoonPies to stranded people. The copyrighted cartoon is reprinted here by permission.

The MP Cultural Club in Charlotte was a frequent Day Sponsor on WDAV, the classical music station operated by Davidson College in Davidson, North Carolina. The broadcast slogan was "Sponsored by the MoonPie Cultural Club, dedicated to bringing culture and humor to the world." No personal names were mentioned, in order not to distract from the significance of the slogan.

Interest in the MoonPie as both a delicious snack and a serious statement of regional culture reached a new level in 1985. Television coverage began when local station WBTV in Charlotte, North Carolina, broadcast MoonPie Patio Picnics that summer.

CNN produced a story about the MoonPie in 1994. Jed Mescon of Chattanooga used his creative genius and perseverance to make a classic video documentary about the MoonPie. Thus CNN was able to send the good news about one of mankind's greatest creations to the hungry multitudes across the nation.

Television station WFMY-TV in Greensboro, North Carolina, aired a story about the MoonPie in 1996. The Voice of America broadcast the story of the MoonPie around the globe in 1999.

In 2000, Turner South Network produced a feature story about the MoonPie for its "Liars & Legends" television series. It broadcast the story hundreds of times.

In 2001, budding filmmaker Emily Ley-Shiley produced the film *How Chattanooga Mooned America*. She explored the history, culture, etiquette, and vast folklore associated with the MoonPie. This delightfully humorous film ended with a burst of brilliance. She showed a full moon gradually changing to a portrait of the snack's creator, Earl W. Mitchell, Sr., of Knoxville, Tennessee. South Carolina Educational Television has shown her film dozens of times.

The MP Cultural Club Charlotte chapter also participated in National Public Radio broadcasts in 2003.

There was no doubt that the humble MoonPie had become a star in 1996, when the American Dairy Council featured it in its "Got Milk?" billboard campaign. The Lo-Fat MoonPie that appeared in it was discontinued by 2005.

In October 2009, *Southern Living* published ideas for decorating MoonPies for after-school snacks and even for Halloween parties. These "frighteningly delicious recipes" included making owl faces using M&Ms, sprinkles, melted chocolate, and candy corn for beaks.

Two annual events associated with the MoonPie are the World Championship MoonPie Eating Contest in Oneonta,

Alabama, and the RC & MoonPie Festival in Bell Buckle, Tennessee. For those who can't get enough of a good thing, these events are a source of great joy.

The World Championship MoonPie Eating Contest is usually held in October of each year, after the summer heat moderates. It takes place in the parking lot of the Walmart store. A Walmart employee, Rodney, returned in 1985 as the reigning champion. He arrived in a stretch limousine, accompanied by two lovely ladies. When he got out of the car, an assistant handed him his top hat and formal coat. Before he was seated, he handed his hat and coat to the assistants. The crowd screamed, "Rodney, Rodney, Rodney," and clapped thunderously to honor their champion. When a college boy beat the champion ten minutes later, the stunned, speechless throng soon emptied the parking lot. CNN reported this important event to America.

Mort Hurst of North Carolina won the championship in 1989.

The world's largest MoonPie festival is held in Bell Buckle, Tennessee, each June. It features a full day of festivities including the MoonPie Parade, the coronation of a king and queen, a ten-mile run, and a concert and ends with the cutting and serving up of the world's largest MoonPie. The tenth annual celebration in 2004 included eighty arts and crafts exhibits and twenty food booths featuring Southern fare such as Tennessee smoked barbeque, hand-squeezed lemonade, and deep-fried MoonPies. A schedule of events can be viewed on the town's Chamber of Commerce Web site.

Champion of the MoonPie Awards

These awards are presented to persons who have shown outstanding creativity in and dedication to spreading the news about the MoonPie. Winners are encouraged to frame the Champion of the MoonPie certificate and hang it beside their Pulitzer, Nobel, and other awards of equal importance.

The ribbons are colored red, white, and blue by a professional artist before the certificate is presented to the recipient. The circle is colored gold.

The number of champions is limited to a dozen living persons. The awards are presented in a private ceremony. This was decided after some unworthy candidates raised a furor over their rejection.

The MoonPie Television Show

A search is under way to find a suitable producer for the MoonPie television program, tentatively called "The Traveling Man." Based on the lives of the early salesmen who sold MoonPies to the far corners of the nation, this program will be a combination of drama and humor. Scenes will be filmed in many of the hamlets and cities visited by these brave salesmen, thus appealing to a huge audience. It will show the drama and hardships faced by these intrepid men, but it will also display their sense of humor as they met the challenges of their chosen profession. Many leading actors are expected to apply for parts in this exciting new show. The most difficult job will be finding writers who have the necessary skill and wit for such an inspiring program.

Numerous Hollywood producers are currently considering additional television programs based on the noble snack. One devoted reader, taking time from his busy day in the television industry, sent in the following.

> I have turned my professional attentions to your MoonPie television show. Rather than "The Traveling Man," the title of which, in my opinion, will not draw the viewers away from such staples as "Dukes of Hazzard" and "The Fall Guy," I humbly submit the following listings for your consideration:
>
> "Magnum, P. I. E."—An action-packed hour featuring Tom Selleck as Magnum, a likeable private eye with crumbs in his moustache, as he chases all over Maui after the elusive evil genius Wo Fat, who has surreptitiously obtained the free world rights to the fabled "Pineapple Pie" formula.
>
> "60 MoonPies"—A hard-hitting, in-depth probe, using hidden cameras and microphones, into the epicurean habits of hosts Steve Kroft, Lesley Stahl, Bob Simon, Katie Couric, and Scott Pelley. One particularly graphic sequence, filmed with a camera hidden in a Coca-Cola cooler under a pile of frozen Zero Bars, depicts one of them not only ripping off the MoonPie wrapper with his teeth but then washing down the noble snack with a cup of cold Colombian coffee. The program is rounded

out by "A Few Minutes with Andy Rooney." (Warning: Parental Guidance—Some portions may be considered unsuitable for younger viewers.)

"M * O * O * N"—A comedy set in the early 1950s depicting the lives and loves of a ragtag bunch of gonzo bakers, whose job it is to repair broken MoonPies, repackage them, and get them back on the shelves of Piggly Wiggly and Winn-Dixie stores as soon as possible. Alan Alda produces, directs, writes, stars, films, edits, scores, lights, moves props, does makeup and hair, caters, and serves as legal advisor in this CBS series.

"The P-Team"—Merriment and mischief abound in this fast-moving adventure series about a crack team of Grenada Island vets who, for a price, travel the world, bringing the noble snack to the oppressed and Pie-less. Led by George Pieppard, the group gets into one zany scrape after another, only to be pulled out at the last minute by the irascible but loveable "Mr. P." ("I just love it when an Original Marshmallow Sandwich comes together.")

Other programs for consideration might include: "Family Pies," "One Pie at a Time," "King Street Blues," "Fantasy Pieland," and of course the daytime drama "One Pie to Give."
—D. G. Smart

MoonPies and the Silver Screen

MoonPies played crucial roles in three classic Hollywood scenes. However, the original scenes were later altered. Remember when Mae West turned to W. C. Fields and asked, "Is that a pistol in your pocket, or are you just glad to see me?" Fields' first answer was: "Actually it's a melliferous MoonPie. Why don't we go up to your place and share the ambrosial morsel?"

Movie trivia buffs have long known that originally it was not a black statue of a common bird of prey that Humphrey Bogart (alias Sam Spade) searched for in the script of *The Maltese Falcon* but rather that of a chocolate MoonPie in Dashiell Hammett's (you guessed it) *The Maltese MoonPie*. The change was made after a break on the set one day when

Bogie turned to a script writer who was nibbling a MoonPie and said, "You sorry wimp! You eat like a bird!"

And finally, it can now be revealed for the first time that one of history's great movie mysteries originally involved MoonPies. In the first draft of the screenplay for *Citizen Kane*, Orson Welles' dying word was, "MoonPie." Since so many people were familiar with the noble snack, however, the director decided that a more obscure final word was appropriate, thus the enduring "Rosebud."

Famous Journalists and the MoonPie

Two popular journalists ceaselessly promoted the MoonPie.

The late Jim Shumaker taught journalism at the University of North Carolina at Chapel Hill, trying desperately, perhaps futilely, to impart some knowledge of grammar, spelling, and composition to students who generally are ignorant of these matters. Perhaps in an effort to keep his sanity, he also wrote a column for the *Charlotte Observer*. Mr. Shumaker was widely known for strictly reporting the facts and never embellishing them. His lively columns depicted the antics of students as they strove to maintain the school's reputation as the beer-drinking capital of the nation while frittering away some time in academic pursuits.

After living near the university for many years, he retreated from the battlefield of objective reporting to Caswell Beach, North Carolina. This is as far from Chapel Hill as you can get in North Carolina without being under the Atlantic Ocean. In keeping with his meager salary, a diet of MoonPies and Pepsis sustained him over the years.

When he received the original manuscript for this book, he encouraged the author to get it published for the enjoyment of mankind everywhere. His references to the noble snack were always correct—he deserved a medal of merit. He passed away on December 19, 2000.

At his memorial service, a speaker proclaimed that Mr. Shumaker loved two things in life: good writing and MoonPies. He then pointed to a table in the rear of the auditorium that was covered with a mountain of chocolate MoonPies and invited the audience to take one as a memento of the occasion.

The late Lewis Grizzard, a widely published columnist for the *Atlanta Journal-Constitution,* came from Georgia, a state whose greatest contribution to the world was the invention of Coca-Cola. (He strived mightily to overcome the handicap of his humble origins.) Mr. Grizzard occasionally mentioned enjoying a MoonPie and soft drink. But for many years he seemed unaware that the name "MoonPie" was a registered trademark and could refer only to the products of the Chattanooga Bakery. Of course, the MoonPie Patrol fired off a letter to enlighten this Southern Scribe and show him the error of his ways. Much to his credit, Mr. Grizzard immediately thereafter started using the name correctly. In a 1984 article, he deplored that he could not gain weight. Evidently, he needed to read the diet guide section of this handbook to see how MoonPies can solve his problem. A copy was sent to him, and we eagerly awaited a reply for the next edition, but it never arrived.

The Jim Bakker Trial

In the late 1980s, on the last day of the trial of this fallen television evangelist at the Federal Courthouse in Charlotte, the Reverend Will B. Dunn, a.k.a. Ron Dickson, passed out 200 MoonPies to the news media who had stood on the lawn since 7:30 a.m. The Reverend Will B. Dunn was a character in Doug Marlette's cartoon strip, "Kudzu," and Ron was dressed in like attire. Providing the MoonPies was a considerate, humane gesture to these dedicated but hungry people.

Some reporters actually called out, "Reverend Dunn! It's so nice to see you."

"Bless you, my son," he replied. "I have come to minister to your bodily needs. May Brother Bakker tend to your spiritual needs."

CNN asked the reverend and his companion, Tracy Simpson, a pretty young lady and devoted member of the MoonPie/Dunn Congregation, for an interview. Tracy wanted to decline, but the reverend assured her that the bored reporters just wished to talk to an attractive girl and likely would not turn on the camera.

When a reporter asked him who he really was, Dickson replied, "Sir, I am the Reverend Will B. Dunn."

The reporter asked his lovely assistant the same question, and Tracy also replied, "Today he really is the Reverend Dunn." CNN showed the interview on its 11:00 p.m. EST broadcast all over America.

A couple of years later, when Jim Bakker returned to the courthouse to get his sentence reduced, the reverend Dunn reappeared. Many reporters greeted him warmly, "How nice to see you again!"

When the reverend tried to give a box of MoonPies to the federal marshal guarding the entrance to the courthouse, the marshal declined, saying he could not accept gifts. The reverend asked if he had to inspect all packages going into the courthouse, and the marshal said yes. "Well, I want to go in with this box that is tied with red, white, and blue ribbon as a show of appreciation for your efforts in preventing gunfire and any attempt to rescue Jim Bakker." He handed the box to the marshal, who smiled in gratitude. The reverend turned and left before the marshal could think of a reply.

When Doug Marlette scheduled a book signing at the Intimate Bookshop in the SouthPark Mall in Charlotte, North Carolina, the author made arrangements with the manager to appear dressed as the reverend Dunn accompanied by 200 MoonPies. The reverend stood outside the entrance and invited people to come in to "meet the famous Doug Marlette and get a free MoonPie." Soon there was a long line of customers waiting for Marlette to sign their copies of his latest book. The manager said it was the best book signing event she had ever seen.

CHAPTER 3

MoonPie Madness

Marion Hankins, a lovely, sophisticated lady, moved to North Carolina after living most of her life in a culturally deprived part of the country. Her colleague, the author, introduced her to MoonPies.

Shortly thereafter, she was inspired to send the following epistle to the Cultural Club's World Headquarters (WHQ).

HOW MOONPIES CHANGED MY LIFE (A TESTIMONIAL)
My friends:
I am here today to tell you how MoonPies changed my life. How the Reverend Mr. Dickson reached down his hand to me, mired in my uncultured existence, and gave me a MoonPie. Now, friends, that may not seem like an earth-shattering event, but I want you to know that the Lord works in mysterious ways, and I truly believe that Mr. Dickson's mission that day was to bring me up out of my ignorance and show me the light of true salvation.

Hear what I'm saying to you!

Before that momentous day, I didn't know even the basics of Southern life. Didn't know "slaw" from "coleslaw." Didn't know from iced tea, country ham, or Luck's® beans. Couldn't go into a respectable restaurant without embarrassing myself. Couldn't even speak the language. I said "could" instead of "might could." Didn't realize that "pen" and "pin" are pronounced exactly the same way. I "pressed" keys instead of "mashing" them. I could go on, friends, but hot tears of embarrassment prevent me.

But on that day—that glorious, MoonPie-in-the-sky day—things changed. I came into the office no wiser than before.

I had had a premonition that there was something in the air, but I figured that it was just the waste treatment facility over on Tvola Road. Little did I know!

Then I saw the notice on the board about a shipment of MoonPies that had come in fresh from Chattanooga (I had to look it up on a map). I've always been one to try anything once, so I shuffled on down to Mr. Dickson's office and plunked down my money. I walked out with a box of Moon-Pies, wondering all the while what the big deal was.

Back at my desk I sat down, broke open the box, and pulled out a MoonPie. That tingling sensation in my fingers should have warned me of what was in store. I ripped open the cellophane and the fragrance of cocoa came wafting up into my nose. For fifteen minutes I just sat there, savoring the heavenly odor.

Then I took a bite. Glory be! My eyes bugged out, my nostrils flared, my teeth tingled, and my heart fluttered. This—this was what it was all about! The revelation tore the veil from my eyes and I saw! Oh, how sweet the taste of cultural salvation!

Today I speak, eat, and even drive a car like a born-again Southerner! And everywhere I preach the glories of Moon-Pies to the heathens, gaining converts and bearing witness to the goodness of the Reverend Mr. Dickson, who helped me out of my misery. Why, just this past month I made a pilgrimage to Bayonne, New Jersey, where I preached a sermon on MoonPies before a congregation of thousands. No fewer than 6,000 people bought boxes of MoonPies before the evening ended. And next week I'll be traveling to Cleveland and then on to Waukesha, Michigan, for a midnight MoonPie rally. I understand that representatives from grocery store and vending machine suppliers all over the world will be in attendance.

Yes, I've come a long way, baby. I have dropped my old life like a mantle from my shoulders. If all of you out there hear my words and believe—really, really believe—then I want to hear you shout, "Hallelujah!" Make a joyful noise, brethren, for you have seen the light! Go forth and bear witness likewise, that those with eyes may see, and those with taste buds may taste, and those with money may buy the fruit of the tree of Chattanooga.

Praise the Pie and pass the RC Cola®!

A Pilgrim's Visit to the Bakery

Following is a report received from a loyal fan who finally realized a lifelong ambition.

Many people grow up, and indeed sometimes grow old, dreaming of faraway places and cities of splendor. Some long for the fabled ambience of Paris in the spring, while others dream of the bustling sophistication of New York. As for me, I have always been in love with the city of Chattanooga, Tennessee. Without question, no other place on earth could ever provide the allure of this legendary birthplace of the MoonPie.

And so it came to pass that one fine day I journeyed to that place of childhood dreams. After passing the old train station that is now a museum for the Chattanooga Choo-Choo, I turned on King Street and spied a simple white building about a block away. As I drew near, I was impressed by the sturdy, neat appearance of this building, constructed so long ago. Then, I mused, there was real pride in using durable materials in a practical design.

Standing in the parking lot across the street, I inhaled deeply, savoring the aroma of baking cookies. Suddenly, I realized that I was looking at the Site of the Creation of the First MoonPie. A feeling of awe swept over me. Slowly, and with a sense of rising excitement, I walked toward the entrance.

On the front of the building, only a small, elegant bronze plaque marked this site as the end of my journey. It simply read: *Chattanooga Bakery*. There are no gaudy signs advertising the purpose or heritage of the structure. Undoubtedly, when the Chattanooga Choo-Choo was first placed on exhibit, hordes of tourists swarmed into the Bakery for tours and free samples, thus totally disrupting production. Therefore, nowhere on the exterior of the building does the word *MoonPie* appear.

Inside, I was greeted warmly and issued a baseball cap bearing the familiar MoonPie emblem—the tour was about to begin. During the next two hours, I witnessed MoonPie mixers masterfully kneading the dough, giant cookie cutters carving that famous shape, mammoth marshmallow machines squirting their gooey goodness, and a packaging machine deftly wrapping the freshly baked pies. A conveyer belt carried a seemingly endless line of boxes down to the loading dock for immediate shipment to grocery stores throughout the country. Never could I have imagined such a display of technology and culinary wizardry all rolled into one.

To be sure, the entire building is cleverly used for the utmost efficiency. There are conveyor belts that double back and forth upon themselves. Boxes for pies are stacked neatly in idle corners. Every nook and cranny of the structure is devoted to that single most noble purpose. In the wintertime, even the hot air, fresh from the 100-foot-long oven, is piped directly into the offices, where the staff is warmed and tantalized by the delicate aromas.

As my official tour ended, I thought back to my childhood days when I dreamed about someday visiting this wonderful shrine. How many MoonPies had I eaten since those days? How many RC Colas had I downed? The scent of a still-warm Double Decker lingered upon my fingers. Nowhere else in the whole world could anyone enjoy a fresher, more delicious MoonPie.

Note: The Bakery later moved to a much larger facility.

MoonPie fans have also sent in the following tips for enjoying the noble snack.

From Granny Marie Davis in Georgia: "I put the MoonPie in the microwave and set the timer for one minute. When the wrapper blows up, I eat it with a spoon."

From Tracy Simpson in North Carolina: "As a youngster I worked on a cotton farm in the summer. At lunch I rode my bicycle about a mile to a country store and bought a bunch of soft drinks and MoonPies. I wrapped an old towel around the drinks to keep them cold. Then we sat under a shade tree and enjoyed lunch."

From Wayne Snyder in North Carolina: "I delivered the afternoon paper when I was a kid. I stopped at Jones Grocery, midway through my route, and bought a MoonPie for a nickel. Then a minute later I bought an RC Cola for a nickel, thus saving the penny tax on a ten cent purchase. I did this six times a week for about six years until I finished high school."

From Phil Furr in North Carolina: "When I worked in a cotton mill in the 1940s, the 'dope wagon' rolled through the mill on a regular basis. That's when Coca-Cola and other soft drinks contained cocaine, hence the name 'dope wagon.' With a dime I bought a MoonPie and a big soft drink. This provided a burst of energy to keep me going at a fast pace."

Kate Campbell is a familiar name to country music fans everywhere. Her second release, called "MoonPie Dreams," was nominated for Folk Album of the Year at the 1997 Nashville Music Awards. It remains one of her finest achievements—and, of course, a favorite selection for true fans of the MoonPie.

After this book was first published, dozens of civic clubs, schools, and church groups asked the author to speak about the benefits of humor and MoonPies in life. He created a slide show that was narrated by Mindy Carnell, a distinguished British lady with impeccable diction. Later, Ellie Perzel narrated an updated version. (The text of a typical speech is in the appendix.)

MoonPies and Kids

In Brooklyn, New York, Sarah Lindberg, age six, used chocolate and vanilla Mini MoonPies to teach classmates how to count to 100. Then the children divided the MoonPies into baskets of twenty snacks and delivered them to other classes. Thus, they learned to share as well as count.

Children can stack MoonPies to build a castle. This can celebrate a birthday, the end of the school year, and other important events.

Dr. Marcus Weaver and his wife, Tammy, of Mooresville, North Carolina, reported that fifteen hungry teenagers at their home had a contest for the most creative way of eating MoonPies. One ate the top off; another opened the MoonPie and ate the marshmallow, like eating the filling of an Oreo® cookie; another took tiny nibbles, like a squirrel; another ate the pie in three huge bites; and so on.

The MoonPie Minstrels

After some diligent research, talented Charlotte musician Ms. P. J. Brunson discovered the original words to some popular songs. For example, she learned that "You Are My Sunshine" was initially called "You Are My MoonPie," but people living above the Mason-Dixon Line at the time didn't know what a MoonPie was. She found that the artists who wrote the songs had been forced to change their lyrics to something generic (such as "sunshine") so that people outside the South might better identify with their work.

Ms. Brunson and her friend Ms. Julie McKeel joined forces to perform these old standards in their original form (and to create new hits). They were designated the Official MoonPie Minstrels, and their concerts were enjoyed by young and old alike. Some of the songs performed by the MoonPie Minstrels are reprinted here.

Chattanooga MoonPie
(Sung to the tune of "Chattanooga Choo-Choo")

Pardon me, boy, is that a Chattanooga MoonPie?
The best in the land—gee, it looks grand!
This ain't a ploy, I'd love a Chattanooga MoonPie.
Fresh from the box, I'd trade you my socks.

I remember bein' just a tyke upon my daddy's knee,
A MoonPie stuffed into my mouth along with Are-rah Cee.
Dinner in the diner couldn't have been finer,
Thanks to the chef who served MoonPie fricassee.

Pardon me, boy, is that a Chattanooga MoonPie?
Oh, it smells so divine, I wish it were mine.
Now don't get annoyed, I need a Chattanooga MoonPie.
Marshmallow inside, a taste you can't hide.

You Are My MoonPie
(Sung to the tune of "You Are My Sunshine")

You are my MoonPie, my only MoonPie.
You make me happy when skies are gray.
You'll never know, dear, how much I love you.
Please don't take my MoonPie away.

(*Once*)
Will the MoonPie be unbroken?
By and by, Lord, by and by,
There's a better home awaitin'
With a MoonPie in the sky. (*second time slower*)

Ballad of the Unknown Salesman
(Sung to the tune of "Ballad of New Orleans")

In 1917 he took that fateful trip
To the Chattanooga Bakery

With a handy little tip:
"Ya take two cookies
And ya coat 'em up with goo,
Put a 'mallow in the middle
And ya might sell one or two."

Chorus: We made them pies and the orders started comin',
     Twice as many as there was a while ago.
     Made some more and they began a-sellin',
     From north of Mississippi to the Gulf of Mexico.

He left that day never to return.
Though they tried a hundred times
His name they never learned.
His pies will live forever
And of this I am sure:
His place will be remembered
In the halls of MoonPie lore!

Chorus: We made them pies and the orders started comin',
     Twice as many as there was a while ago.
     Made some more and they began a-sellin',
     From north of Mississippi to the Gulf of Mexico.

Driver of the Pies
(Sung to the tune of "Leader of the Pack")

They were always putting him down.
    (down, down)
He delivered MoonPies all over town.
    (Yes, he drove them all over town.)
I don't care about their lies,
'Cause I know that in my eyes,
He'll always be my Driver of the Pies.

They said he tried to hijack a load
    (load, load)

That dreadful night he ran off the road.
    (Yes he did, he drove it off the road)
But I was there late that night,
When he reached for his last bite.
You're gone forever, Driver of the Pies.

Spoken part:
They say some things are not meant to be,
The future is not always ours to see.
I watched our dreams turn to ash
When he swerved to miss a 1958 Nash.
My heart lies broken, Driver of the Pies.

He died that night out on the street.
    (street, street)
His morning rounds he'd never keep.
    (Oh no, his rounds he would never keep.)
Every time I smell a MoonPie

I can't help but break down and cry.
I'll always love you, Driver of the Pies.

The Official MoonPie Ballad

He was a hungry salesman on the road and all alone,
Looking for a taste that he could call his very own.
Fate was smiling on him when he stopped that summer day,
When his vision of a MoonPie seemed so far away.
But great things started happening right there in Tennessee
And soon in Chattanooga rose the MoonPie factory.

Chorus: He wanted MoonPies . . . MoonPies . . .

The story spread for miles around, the MoonPie gathered fame,
Thanks to a hungry salesman who wouldn't settle for the same.
From Birmingham to Raleigh, the news spread far and wide;
The South was rising up and the MoonPie riding high.
It became a central part of Southern hospitality,
The best we had to offer to a world so much in need.

Chorus: They wanted MoonPies . . . MoonPies . . .

Now in the heart of our old South, believers gather 'round
To share another MoonPie and raise this joyous sound.
Anyone can find it, it's not that hard to see,
Just have yourself a MoonPie, join our happy family.
Well, that's a little history but the story's just begun.
The passion is still rising and the MoonPie's moving on.
Millions gather everyday to spread this Southern cheer
And share their love of MoonPies with those they hold so dear.

Chorus: We wanted MoonPies . . . MoonPies . . .

So listen, children, gather 'round and a story you shall hear
Of how the traveling salesman left us all with MoonPie cheer.

(*Slower*) So raise your RC Colas®, toast his precious name,
And sing this song of Moon Pies—sing it once again!

Chorus: He wanted MoonPies . . . MoonPies . . .
He wanted MoonPies . . . MoonPies . . .

The MoonPie Medley

(*Twice*)
It's been a too long time with no MoonPie,
And I'm ready for a chocolate Double Decker.

(*Twice*)
Can't you see, oh can't you see
What that MoonPie, it's being doin' to me?

(*Once*)
I'm being followed by a MoonPie, MoonPie, MoonPie.
Skippin' and hoppin' on a MoonPie, MoonPie, MoonPie.

CHAPTER 4

Savoring the Noble Snack

Obviously the best part of the MoonPie experience is eating it. It's an experience decidedly unique to each individual—it defies description. To achieve full enjoyment of the delightful MoonPie, it is highly recommended to follow the rules of proper etiquette at all times. Use of the guidelines presented in this chapter will maximize the overall experience to the point of speechless joy (you'll soon discover that there's little point in trying to speak with a mouth full of MoonPie).

Proper MoonPie Etiquette

The following information, excerpted from *The Definitive Guide to MoonPie Etiquette,* by Victoria Winthrop, was gathered from numerous interviews with some of the most cultured and educated people available, all with intimate knowledge of the subject.

Mood and Setting

MoonPies are proper fare for any occasion, public or private, although the most civilized people never serve it before 10 a.m. True connoisseurs prefer quiet, dimly lit settings.

The highest level of MoonPie enjoyment is obtained during times of quiet reflection, yet sharing a MoonPie with a

loved one can create one of life's most tender moments. This snack, however, can be enjoyed almost anywhere, at any time, by anyone with teeth. It is possible to enjoy them without teeth, but it's much easier with the proper choppers.

As the MoonPie tends to crumble, it is not recommended for consumption in bed. Refraining from such activities ensures one's comfort between the sheets (and the comfort of any visitors one may have).

Opening the MoonPie

The wrapper should be opened gently by pulling it apart at one end, starting in the center with fingers on opposite sides. Grasp the front of the wrapper near the top, just above the MoonPie logo, with the left thumb and forefinger. Hold the seam on the back, opposite the left-hand fingers, with the right thumb and forefinger. Press the two thumbs together at the knuckle. They will act as a hinge and allow you to pull the wrapper open with perfect control. Using the thumbs as a pivot point is the secret to success.

This method is clever and leaves an opening to push out the MoonPie a little at a time while consuming the snack, eliminating the need for a finger bowl afterwards. Conversely, if one's hands are soiled, the wrapper protects the MoonPie.

Immediately after opening the wrapper, deeply inhale the delicate fragrance, which may be rich chocolate, ripe banana, tempting vanilla, luscious orange, tart lemon, or romantic strawberry. Hold the package with the MoonPie name facing away from you so that passersby can see that you are eating the real thing, not a cheap imitation.

It is considered extremely bad manners to rip open the wrapper in a haphazard manner. Wrapper-rippers are obviously ignorant of the finer points of etiquette and should therefore be avoided in social situations.

Taking the Bite

Most authorities agree that the MoonPie is best enjoyed in large bites—the larger the bite, the greater the enjoyment. Small bites do not seem to yield the same effect. Falling crumbs should be ignored until the snack and accompanying beverage are finished. All the crumbs should then be brushed off discreetly, except for the larger crumbs, which may secretly be picked up and used for dessert.

The proper way to unwrap and hold the MoonPie

Selecting Complementary Beverages

Traditionally, MoonPies have been eaten while drinking RC Cola® (pronounced ARE-rah Cee), although most other soft drinks are also approved. Some scholars have debated the reasons RC Cola® became so popular an accompaniment to MoonPies. The truth is very simple. When the MoonPie first started to grow in popularity, the RC Cola®, with twelve ounces per bottle, was a better bargain than Coca-Cola®, with only six or so ounces per bottle. Every kid old enough to have an allowance figured this out pretty fast.

Double Cola® and Cheerwine® are included on the approved list, but it is difficult to locate them in some parts of the world. Cheerwine®, a delicious cherry-flavored soft drink, is considered the height of elegance when served in a crystal goblet accompanied by a MoonPie. Cheerwine® is bottled by the Carolina Beverage Company in Salisbury, North Carolina, and distributed in North Carolina, South Carolina, Virginia, West Virginia, Georgia, Alabama, Louisiana, Tennessee, Texas, Oklahoma, Norway, and Sweden. Nehi® orange soda is also wonderful with a MoonPie. In the South, folks often call this combination the "Big Orange Belly Washer."

Glass bottles are always preferred over cans for their visual and sensual appeal, but cans are acceptable if bottles cannot be found. The proper method of holding the bottle is subject to debate. Some prefer to grasp the bottle just below the top, thereby enabling a swig with a simple movement of the wrist. Others prefer to hold the bottle by the midsection and get some arm movement into the drinking process. It is approved, however, to change styles while drinking.

Other possible beverage selections include milk, all fruit juices, and hot coffee or tea. Hot beverages are perfect for dissolving the marshmallow and frosting left on teeth.

For formal entertaining, beverages should complement the MoonPie's flavor. A piña colada is delightful with a banana MoonPie. Champagne works well with the vanilla MoonPie, but that combination should be reserved for the evening. A light white wine is excellent during the day, and a robust rose or red wine is considered *de rigueur* at dinner parties or semiformal gatherings. Any carefully selected wine should complement all of the MoonPie flavors.

Proper Cleansing Technique

At least half the beverage should be saved for the cleansing procedure. Carefully take a large drink of the beverage and swish the liquid around in your mouth. During the cleansing process, the lips should be closed and loud, vulgar noises, such as burping, must be avoided. Repeat several times, as necessary.

Leftovers

If part of the snack is to be saved for later, the wrapper should be folded around the remaining part and a rubber band placed around the wrapper to retain freshness.

Wrapper Disposal

When dining in a restaurant, lunchroom, or cafeteria, press the wrapper flat and gently lay it on the table with the word "MoonPie" facing upward to inform all passersby that someone with discriminating taste has dined there.

In other situations, the wrapper should be placed face up in a suitable waste receptacle. Wadding up the wrapper is considered bad form and can completely negate the effect derived from the eating of the MoonPie. Wrapper-rippers and wrapper-wadders are no more civilized than burpers. They display their ignorance and a lack of good manners. Such crude persons should be avoided.

Unacceptable Manners and Uses

There are certain uses of the MoonPie that tradition, decorum, and good manners simply do not permit.

It is not acceptable to peel apart the cookies and lick the marshmallow filling. This would be a disastrous effort anyway—the cookies invariably crumble.

One should never begin eating a MoonPie and then walk away, leaving the half-eaten pie unattended. This is a direct slap in the face of cultural tradition. Moreover, one should not expect to find the uneaten portion of the MoonPie upon his or her return.

Never use a MoonPie as a bookmark. This not only does a gross injustice to the MoonPie but also destroys the book. Although the activities of reading and eating MoonPies are in themselves pleasurable, the two should never be combined in this manner.

It is not proper to offer a friend an unwrapped MoonPie that has accidentally fallen to the ground. Instead, dry your eyes and take the soiled MoonPie home, where you can remove the dirt particles one by one in privacy and then enjoy it yourself.

MoonPies are not suitable for use as earmuffs. Although the appearance is quite chic, they're not heavy enough to provide much warmth and the practice could lead to frosting-coated ears.

Refrain from throwing a MoonPie even if a friend should ask, "Hey, toss me a MoonPie." The only time a MoonPie should be airborne (other than during the course of a few recreational activities that require you to be airborne as well) is in New Orleans, where millions of specially made Mini MoonPies are thrown during the

annual Mardi Gras celebration. The city has granted special permission for this practice.

The MoonPie should not be used as padding under the garments of thin or under-endowed women. If left in the wrapper, it produces funny crinkling sounds at the most inopportune times; if it is removed from the wrapper, body warmth usually melts the frosting and makes for messy clothes (or kinky activities, which the bakery does not endorse).

MoonPies are inappropriate for use in high-altitude jet planes and in deep-sea research vessels. At high altitudes, loss of cabin pressure will explode the MoonPie wrapper and spread frosting all over the windshield and instrument panel. At extreme depths, the pressure will flatten the pie to a fraction of its original size and render it inedible, inevitably leading to the bends.

Do not take MoonPies on African safaris. Natives have been known to go bananas over the pies, thus threatening to shorten the trip as well as a few limbs.

Never feed MoonPies to large dogs. If you run out of snacks before they run out of appetite, serious bodily harm could result.

Do not eat a MoonPie while singing the National Anthem or while reciting seventeenth-century Italian poetry (if any exists).

Restaurant Dining

Many of the family-style restaurants, such as the PoFolks chain based in Panama City, Florida, now have MoonPies available for dessert. (They are often kept next to the cash register for protection.) Ask the waiter or waitress to bring you a MoonPie sealed in its wrapper so that you can be certain it is the genuine article—not an inferior imitation bearing the impressions of the waitperson's fingerprints. A truly high-class establishment will offer to heat the MoonPie for ten to twelve seconds in a microwave oven, just long enough to bring out the subtle aroma and to soften the marshmallow.

The highlight of an elegant dining experience—a MoonPie for dessert.

Should you choose to dine in an establishment that does not yet offer MoonPies, it's perfectly permissible to bring your own. (Actually, that's where the term brown-bagging originated; at first it was known as pie-bagging.) The MoonPie carrying case, made of crush-proof plastic and closely resembling a Tupperware® sandwich box, is available by special order. It holds two regular MoonPies and fits neatly into a coat pocket or into a lady's handbag.

You may also wish to leave the following comment card with the restaurant owner or manager:

To the Manager: I enjoyed dining in your fine establishment, but was greatly disappointed that you did not offer the genuine MoonPie for dessert. Therefore, I must downgrade your rating from 5 stars to 4 stars. I would appreciate your correcting this deficiency before I dine here again.

Respectfully,

These cards, available through the MoonPie Cultural Club, are printed in blue ink on the finest quality white paper and are packed in boxes of 100. The address of the bakery is on the reverse. A similar card is available to leave in grocery stores when appropriate. The above message is also printed on the back of the club's membership cards. Of course, these cards are only shown to the manager and not left behind, for they are expensive.

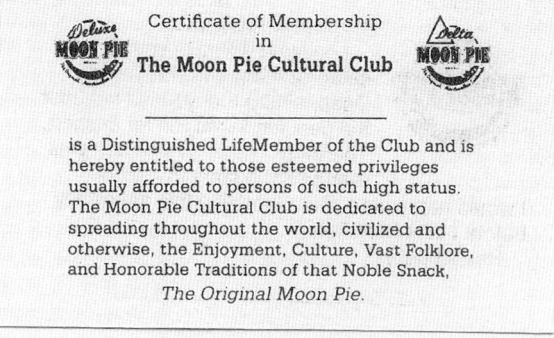

Dining Accessories

The Executive Bib, emblazoned with the MoonPie image, is highly recommended for the office. A few crumbs always fall while savoring the pie, and the bib protects your tie, vest, and trousers or, if appropriate, your cleavage, bosom, and dress. A cleverly designed pocket on the bib will catch the crumbs from dozens of MoonPies. (Carpenters use a similar garment called a nail apron.)

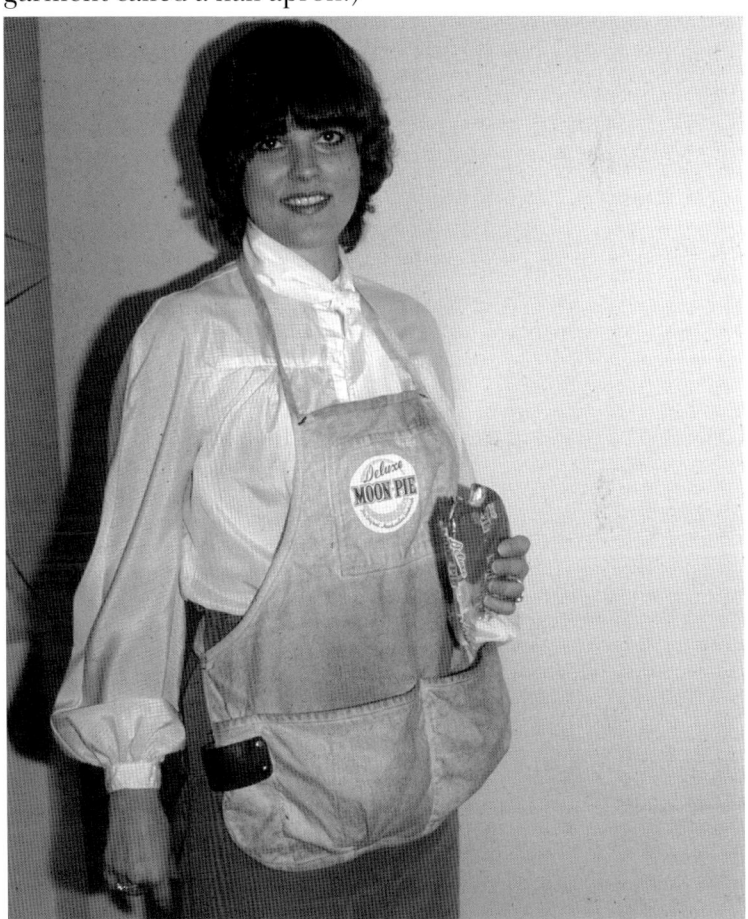

Sarah Lane proudly wearing her MoonPie Executive Bib

The Official MoonPie Napkin, deeply embossed, is available by the gross and adds the finishing touch of elegance to every snack.

Gourmet Desserts

The MoonPie can be a key ingredient in many delicious desserts. The chef is limited only by his/her imagination. The following suggestions are only a starting point for some fantastic creations.

Warmed MoonPies: Remove the wrapper and warm the MoonPie for 10 to 12 seconds in a microwave oven to produce a delicious fragrance. Caution: Do not try this in a regular oven.

MoonPie Jubilee: This is similar to the famous cherries jubilee. Cover a vanilla MoonPie with vanilla ice cream and cherries. Pour on some brandy and ignite. The results are spectacular. Keep a bucket of water handy in case things get out of control.

Flavorings: Using a fork, carefully poke several small holes in the top of a MoonPie. Sprinkle a few drops of food flavoring over the pie. Some popular flavors include lemon, vanilla (for a double vanilla taste on a vanilla pie), almond, orange, cinnamon, crème de menthe, crème de cacao, and rum.

Sauces: Add a tasty sauce of your own creation and serve on a small plate.

Toppings: Add chocolate syrup, honey, chopped nuts, or shredded coconut for a truly exotic treat. Note: Do not add them all at the same time.

Ice cream: Place a scoop of ice cream on top of a MoonPie, microwave for 15 seconds, and serve as a regal delight. At birthdays, put a lighted candle on the ice cream.

The Kids' Delight: Cover a chocolate MoonPie with chunky peanut butter. Heat gently in a microwave oven for 15 seconds.

The Breakfast Beauty: Cover a vanilla MoonPie with butter and blackberry jelly.

Use of the Empty Box

MoonPies are packed in boxes by the dozen. After the twelve MoonPies have been eaten, you can use the box in many ways to show that you are a MoonPie fan.

#1. Fill the empty box with wadded newspapers and seal the lid with cellophane tape. Place the box on the rear window ledge of your car, with the long side of the box facing the back window. Anchor the box to the window ledge with a piece of cellophane tape.

Putting a brick in the empty box is not approved. If you slam on the brakes or otherwise come to an abrupt stop, the brick could damage your windshield, upholstery, hairstyle, etc.

Be sure to replace the box before the sun fades the printing.

Some of the more creative MoonPie fans have mounted their empty boxes on springs so that the box bobs from side to side when the car is in motion. Others have connected their brake lights to a bulb inside the box. Each time the brakes are applied, the box is illuminated. This technique is particularly popular in L.A. (Lower Alabama).

#2. Cut out the largest MoonPie logo on the box lid and punch a hole at the top center. Moisten a plastic, hooked suction cup with a bit of petroleum jelly, such as Vaseline®, and stick it on the rear window behind the driver. Hang the MoonPie logo from the hook, bending the hook with a pair of pliers to hold the logo securely. Save the other logos on the box as replacements for when the first one fades.

Show others that you are a person of good taste or that you were . . .

#3. Cut out a small logo and tape it on the forward side of your rearview mirror, being careful not to obstruct your view.

In addition to being subtle means of demonstrating your good taste and refinement to the rest of the motoring public, the logos will help you find your car in a crowded parking lot.

#4. You can make a colorful mobile by suspending several boxes from strings running through the ends of the boxes. This lets the boxes hang in a stable condition.

#5. You can glue the pictures and words from several boxes to a larger cardboard box to build an impressive model of a monument to the "unknown salesman," who created the first MoonPie.

CHAPTER 5

The Sensuous Woman and MoonPies

What is a sensuous woman and what is it exactly that sets her apart from her sisters? She is a woman who loves candlelight, soft music, and fine perfumes; a woman who delights in the soft touch of satin and lace; and a woman with a sense of adventure who revels in games between the sexes. More than this, she's a woman who appreciates the delicate allure of the MoonPie and can use her intimate knowledge of its temptations to her advantage when it comes to landing a suitable beau.

The MoonPie as an Invitation to Romance

Since time began, women have skillfully plied their ways among men. A coy glance, a brief touch, a shy smile, and a seductive whisper are all tools of the woman's trade. But the truly sensuous woman has at her disposal a lure so powerful that few men in possession of all their hormones can resist. I speak, of course, of the modern MoonPie. Just how, you may ask, can that most glorious of dessert treats be employed to a romantic end? Consider, dear reader, the following ploys, courtesy of Victoria Winthrop.

The Casual Proffering of a MoonPie

A crowded room, a chance meeting, and an invitation to romance—what sensuous woman doesn't know the feeling

She has a lot to offer—a MoonPie

of suddenly finding herself in the presence of Mr. Right? Yet how does one create that spark, that special moment of communion? The sensuous woman will casually let a MoonPie slip unobtrusively from her purse, only to land near or on the feet of her object of desire. Executed in the proper fashion, this device will prove to be an invaluable addition to the sensuous woman's arsenal.

The Formal Proffering of a MoonPie

Suppose you are in your favorite restaurant when you spy a man who catches your eye. As your solitary meal progresses, you exchange furtive glances from across the room. He smiles shyly while you burn inside. How does the sensuous woman break the ice? Imagine his delight when the waiter delivers a MoonPie along with your personal compliments. His love will surely be yours tonight!

The Personal Display of a Single MoonPie

The more adventurous woman will take a bolder approach to setting the "MoonPie Trap." The personal display of a single MoonPie is often the most powerful bait the sensuous woman can set. A MoonPie tucked jauntily in the cleavage with the top just protruding from one's evening wear is sure to attract the attention of even the most jaded man. Note, however, that care should be taken to leave the MoonPie wrapper securely in place, while those not so well-endowed should refrain from this practice altogether. They could, however, experiment with a Mini MoonPie. (This acceptable use is not to be confused with the unacceptable use of MoonPies as padding.)

The Sensuous Consumption of a MoonPie

While many women find it difficult to express their most intimate feelings, the sensuous woman can communicate volumes with a single act. Take, for example, the sensuous consumption of a MoonPie. By following a few basic rules, a woman can elevate the simple act of eating a MoonPie into a symphony of seduction.

Step 1: As the sensuous woman sits opposite her prey, her first task is to select an appropriate MoonPie. Color is especially important in this respect, and an attempt should be made to complement both complexion and evening attire.

Do: Slide the pie unobtrusively from your purse.

Don't: Line up all flavors and choose in "eeny-meeny-miney-mo" fashion.

Step 2: Gently open the cellophane wrapper in traditional MoonPie fashion. Push the pie slowly through the open wrapper from below until just the top is exposed. Softly blow across the pie so that the enticing aroma wafts toward your intended. The banana flavor is especially effective if this last strategy is employed.

Do: Gently pull the sides of the cellophane wrapper away from each other.

Don't: Rip the top of the package off with your teeth.

Step 3: With eyelids lowered and lips slightly parted, bring the pie slowly to your mouth. While gazing directly into your

The Sensuous Woman and MoonPies

True happiness is a MoonPie and a good woman

intended's eyes, take your first bite, letting the pie linger for a brief moment before you begin to chew.

Do: Look directly into your intended's eyes.

Don't: Make rude eating noises while casting your gaze wildly about the room.

Step 4: To maximize the intended effect, you may want to depart from accepted MoonPie etiquette. That is, instead of washing the remaining morsels away with the appropriate beverage, slowly collect the crumbs from around your lips and teeth with an exaggerated sweep of the tongue. If executed in a precise fashion, this final gesture should seal the fate of your hapless prey.

Do: Use your tongue to remove stubborn particles of MoonPie.

Don't: Wipe your mouth and surrounding facial area with the back of your hand.

The MoonPie as an Accessory to Love

Many women tend to overlook the importance of the MoonPie as an accessory to love. The truly sensuous woman, however, would never consider facing a night of romance without a complete assortment of MoonPies. Furthermore, the use of the MoonPie as an accessory to love is limited only by one's imagination. Some conventional uses of this special aid to romance are explored below.

In the Boudoir

Some may consider the boudoir to be a totally inappropriate setting for something so traditionally wholesome as the MoonPie. Yet wholesomeness is the very quality that most American men are looking for in a woman today. The sensuous woman should keep a fresh assortment of MoonPies in her nightstand. For those truly special occasions, leave a single MoonPie on top of the nightstand so it will be handy to share later on with Mr. Right.

As a "Morning After" Snack

What could be more romantic than rousing your man with breakfast in bed? Freshly brewed coffee, juice, fruit, and, of course, slightly warmed MoonPies served in bed on a lovely breakfast tray will make an indelible impression upon any man. The vanilla pie is far superior to any common pastry. Need I say more?

As a Calling Card

Many a woman has pondered the question of how to make a man remember her after that first mad, passionate encounter. A MoonPie can be just the solution to this problem. When visiting her man at his home, the sensuous woman will leave a MoonPie as a kind of calling card, with her name and phone number clearly written on the wrapper with a permanent marker. Some recommended hiding places for this surprise are under his pillow, in his underwear drawer, or on the seat of his car (passenger side only).

The Complete MoonPie Woman

The sensuous woman will employ every trick at her disposal to attract that special man. When MoonPies are added to her arsenal, the outcome is almost always preordained. No man could possibly resist such a woman. A woman who knows how to entice a man with MoonPies, how to use the MoonPie as an accessory to love, and how to employ MoonPies to keep her man happy is the complete MoonPie woman.

Note: Victoria Winthrop is the pseudonym of Linda Whitener.

CHAPTER 6

The MoonPie Effect

Historically speaking, there's nothing new under the sun. Although the modern MoonPie was created in 1917, that doesn't rule out the possibility that earlier versions of the venerable snack existed since the dawn of mankind. Perhaps lost in the mists of time, it could be that the MoonPie merely made its big comeback in 1917.

This theory would explain why archeologists have discovered so many empty vaults beneath the tombs of the ancient Egyptian pharaohs inside the pyramids. Could it be that these chambers were really MoonPie storage vaults so that the deceased rulers could take their most prized possessions with them into the next life? If that's the case, the vaults were probably emptied by the hordes of hungry workers who built the pyramids—they could have consumed all the MoonPies during their coffee breaks.

There's a remarkable similarity between the empty vaults of the pharaohs and Al Capone's empty vault. The notorious Mr. Capone had access to the more recent version of the MoonPie, and that could be what he had stored inside the vault. How and when his vault was emptied remains a mystery to this day.

Most of today's MoonPie fans have themselves experienced mysterious losses of the noble snack. They tuck their boxes of MoonPies into the most inaccessible reaches of cupboards and sock drawers and on the tops of refrigerators, but when they return to their hiding places, they find only empty boxes. The MoonPies have mysteriously disappeared.

Recent scholarly studies of historical literature have discovered references that tend to support the theory that MoonPies have been around a lot longer than previously thought. The traditional textbook versions of these quotes were found to be incorrect for a variety of reasons. To set the record straight, we present some of the more notable quotations so that the reader can form his or her own opinion about the impact that the MoonPie has had on mankind.

For example, it is recorded in faded documents that Richard III of England actually said, "My kingdom for a MoonPie!" Samuel Johnson later inserted a horse into the quote because he couldn't find "MoonPie" in his dictionary.

Nathan Hale, the great American patriot, obviously was thinking about the starving soldiers when he uttered his famous last words, "I regret that I only have one MoonPie to give for my country." He had only one because MoonPies were not packaged and sold by the dozen until a quarter of the way through the twentieth century.

"The only thing we have to fear . . . is running out of MoonPies" was the challenge that Franklin D. Roosevelt gave to America during the Great Depression. He knew that the nation's wartime productivity depended upon keeping a supply of MoonPies on the farms, in factories, and in offices.

"Let them eat MoonPies!" France's famed Marie Antoinette uttered this sentence (showing her disregard for the welfare of the starving peasants) sometime before she lost her voice, along with her head.

"I shall return . . . for a MoonPie." That was the real reason why Gen. Douglas MacArthur vowed to return to the Philippines during World War II.

"Give me MoonPies or give me death!" was the original battle cry of Patrick Henry during the American Revolution.

On June 17, 1775, at the Battle of Bunker Hill, the Americans were outnumbered and low on ammo. When the British started coming up the hill, Col. William Prescott commanded, "Don't fire until you see the whites of their MoonPies," so that his soldiers wouldn't waste ammo. The British advanced in one line and fired. There were too many British to hold back, and the Americans had to retreat. (Contributed by Lynn Prescott.)

Role in the Building of America

The development of America as a powerful nation did not really begin until after 1917, the year the MoonPie was created. Millions of workmen toiled harder and faster each day, as their morning and afternoon "MoonPie" time approached. This extra spurt of productivity made a tremendous contribution to American industry that until now has not been officially recognized.

Recently, a large international computer company, which wishes to remain anonymous, revealed its secret method of building new offices and computer centers in an incredibly short period of time. One official claimed that the "fast track" record was due entirely to months of meticulous planning, extraordinary attention to details, the use of the Critical Path Method (CPM) on a huge computer, and the brilliant construction management team.

Another official, who really knew what happened, explained it this way:

> That is a bunch of bull. The truth is incredibly simple. The architects and engineers were treated to MoonPie parties as each design project was completed. Never had they designed so well and so fast. When actual construction began, the construction manager, wearing an official MoonPie hard hat and jacket, passed out dozens of MoonPies each day at precisely 9:00 a.m. to the workers. Good humor and a spirit of teamwork—direct results of his action—are what led to the fast completion of the projects.

The MoonPie and Sports

Much has been made recently of nutrition and its role in sports. Some marathon runners, for example, claim that the consumption of large quantities of pasta twenty-four hours before a race provides them with an energy reserve when it is most needed. Boxers and football players, on the other hand, have traditionally eaten large amounts of protein while in training.

The relationship of the MoonPie to popular Southern sports, such as football, horseracing, basketball, soccer, tennis, and even cheerleading and tailgating, is evident. Its use to enhance performance in some less obvious sports is outlined below.

Hang Gliding

Although hang gliding isn't actually considered a competitive sport, a MoonPie is an excellent snack while engaging in this activity. The wrapper may be pre-opened and secured with a rubber band before launching. While you are aloft, you may hold the MoonPie in one hand and rip open the wrapper with your teeth. You must then carefully tuck the wrapper into a pocket and dispose of it properly after landing.

This is one of the few situations where ripping the wrapper open is considered acceptable etiquette. If you were to use both hands to loosen the wrapper, the glider could get out of control and crash to the ground, thus ruining the MoonPie.

An experienced hang glider reports that the height of ecstasy occurs when eating a MoonPie at maximum altitude—soaring free like an eagle.

Future plans call for the sponsorship of a hang glider, with the MoonPie logo emblazoned on the wings. Awards will be given for the highest altitude reached while eating a MoonPie.

Running

While some runners prefer eating spaghetti before a race, research shows that consuming MoonPies will provide the same effect. MoonPies are also neater than most forms of pasta and may be handed, along with a cup of water, to a passing runner. Handing a plate of hot spaghetti to a passing runner is not recommended.

Motorcycling

The MoonPie is an excellent snack to enjoy during short motorcycling trips. MoonPies may be conveniently stored in saddlebags or a backpack. For longer trips, a sidecar will provide adequate MoonPie storage.

We caution the rider to use the opening technique described for hang gliders in order to avoid fatal accidents and a possible flattening of the MoonPie.

Sailing

The MoonPie is the perfect dessert to carry aboard a sailboat. Leaving the MoonPie in its wrapper will protect it from water damage.

If an unopened MoonPie accidentally falls overboard, it will float for several hours and can be used for survival rations should the sailboat capsize. This may not be helpful, however, if sharks are nearby.

MoonPies make excellent emergency rations if a life raft is used to abandon ship.

Skiing

Whether skiing on the water or on snow, you can enjoy a MoonPie for a quick energy boost. Some water-skiers like to tuck a single MoonPie in their bathing suit, where it can be easily retrieved. Similarly, snow skiers will often bury a box of

MoonPies in a snowdrift. MoonPies served with hot chocolate make the perfect après-ski snack.

Ice Hockey

A frozen chocolate Double Decker MoonPie makes an excellent hockey puck. The player scoring a goal gets to keep the puck for a snack after the game, assuming he has any teeth left.

Cycling

The marshmallow from a MoonPie can be used to make a temporary patch in the inner tube of a bicycle tire. Try that with a pack of cheese crackers and see how far you get.

NASCAR

In 1998 and 1999, the Bakery became a marketing partner with NASCAR, which started as a competition among moonshiners with their souped-up cars. The MoonPie logo is emblazoned on the car as well as tattooed on the driver's arms and chest, unless, of course, the driver is a lady. The Bakery soon had to start a second shift to meet the increased demand for its products. This was the first time in nearly a hundred years that the bakery needed a longer workday.

NASCAR benefited from this close association with MoonPies as well. The MoonPie obviously lifted the races from being classified as a "redneck" sport, and attendance soared. Fans, and even drivers, knew that MoonPies were the perfect snack to be enjoyed during the long and exciting races.

CHAPTER 7

Childrearing—The MoonPie Method

MoonPies have an important place in the rearing of children, fitting perfectly into the discipline, motivation, and reward system.

The MoonPie Strongbox, with combination lock, is available to ensure the safety of your inventory. It holds four dozen MoonPies and protects them from children, bugs, mice, and other vermin.

When it comes to the hardest job of all (civilizing one's own offspring), MoonPies can make things a bit easier. The snack can be used to discipline (withholding the MoonPie) or motivate (using the MoonPie to reward good behavior). Other methods such as the "timeout" system have made little impact in producing civilized adults. Well-meaning (but sadly misguided) parents who used the timeout system can now be found posting bail for their wayward youngsters.

The concept of the benevolent dictator works well to keep things moving in the right direction. For this concept to be effective, it should be emphasized that the *parent* must fill the position of dictator. Some parents neglect the MoonPie as a means of positive reinforcement, yet even small children respond without fail to the promise of the irresistible treat. Although some experts disagree about the exact age when children should be introduced to MoonPies, all readily agree that if the child has teeth, the child is old enough for MoonPies, and to be weaned.

One mistake that parents should take care not to make is to leave their supply of MoonPies unguarded. More than one startled parent has returned to the kitchen to find a little one sitting on the floor, surrounded by the remains of what was once a three-month supply of MoonPies.

"I'm starting my baby off right."

This delicious treat should be included in the school lunch bag and taken to movies, football and soccer games, parties, etc. It is the perfect snack for Boy Scouts and Girl Scouts on hikes and camping trips. Imagine the thrill of sharing a MoonPie in the woods with a Scout of the opposite sex.

MoonPies are especially suited for family road trips. When the youngsters tire of video games and other high-tech diversions, it's time to break out the MoonPies to preserve whatever shred of parental sanity might be left after several hundred miles of family togetherness.

The MoonPie method of positive behavior reinforcement has proven its effectiveness since its introduction in 1917. Parents have used MoonPies for generations to help them rear happy and well-adjusted—not to mention well-fed—children. For this reward system to remain effective, it's very important that the parents don't run out of MoonPies. Desirable behavior and family harmony could start to deteriorate rapidly if that should happen.

Dr. Wilhelm M. Clarke declared the following in an article entitled "MoonPies in the Rearing of Children and Other Wild Creatures," which appeared in *International Journal of Child Psychology*: "Today, child psychologists the world over are discovering the value of MoonPies as an educational tool. At a recent conference in Vienna, concerning the place of MoonPies in the education of children, Professor Hemple von Stumpledorf stated: "Vittout zee MoonPie, zee art of childrent razink iz gerstunkin." Although many scholars disagree over the exact translation of Professor von Stumpledorf's statement, the intent of his proclamation remains clear."

The Withholding of MoonPies as Punishment

An equally important strategy in the rearing of children is the calculated withholding of MoonPies in the face of undesirable behavior. Again, parents either neglect or fail to understand the irresistible hold that MoonPies have over children. A child raised on a consistent program of MoonPie reinforcement will quickly demonstrate "acceptable behavior" when suddenly faced with total deprivation. In a case study reported in the *Journal of Motivational Learning*, a seventeen-year-old illiterate learned to read and write in seventy-two hours after being given a simple choice: read and write, or no more MoonPies.

Parents all over the world are adopting MoonPie conditioning as an alternative to traditional forms of behavior modification. To be sure, the effectiveness of a spanking or verbal harangue pales in comparison to the MoonPie approach. Perhaps Professor von Stumpledorf best summed it up when he told the Vienna conference, "Spare zee Pie undt spoil zee childt."

In an experiment conducted at the University of Boogertown, North Carolina, it was clearly demonstrated that monkeys and small rodents learned up to 75 percent faster when introduced to a strict regimen of MoonPie reinforcement. The experiment was set up in the following manner. One group of subjects, the control group, was continually rewarded with unlimited food, mild electrical stimuli to the brain's pleasure zones, and unlimited sex. The MoonPie group, on the other hand, was simply rewarded with assorted pieces of MoonPies. At the conclusion of the experiment, the control group remained happy but relatively stupid.

The MoonPie group, however, demonstrated incredible leaps of intellect. While the mice learned to run the most complex mazes designed by the university's Psychology Department, some of the monkeys eventually learned to communicate with the undergraduates, something the dean of students has never been able to do. In a more recent development, two of the apes have applied for admission at the University of Boogertown and have a good chance of being admitted.

In the experiment, the results of withdrawal of rewards were both startling and dramatic.

When rewards were withheld from the control group, those subjects simply wandered off to fall asleep or collected in small groups to indulge in small talk.

When MoonPies were withheld from the second group, those subjects reacted in a much more agitated manner. Among the mice, there were random riots and at least one planned demonstration. The monkeys, however, reacted even more violently. Two of the apes regrettably took their own lives while a third sent threatening notes to the president of the university.

CHAPTER 8

MoonPie Over My Hammy

As chapter 4 attests, the possibilities for serving MoonPies are endless. In fact, some people have found the pleasure so overwhelming that they've been unable to control their appetites. The result often is split seams in clothing and broken springs in cars. For those who have overindulged in MoonPie pleasure, the MoonPie Diet can turn things around. As with any diet, it's a good idea to start off by consulting your doctor and counting calories.

MoonPie Calories

Regular MoonPie = 220 calories
Mini MoonPie = 152 calories
Double Decker MoonPie = 330 calories
(a small price to pay for such joy)

The MoonPie Diet can help people get in better physical condition and have fun doing it. Most diet plans are dull as bran flakes and offer nothing to look forward to, but this diet presents exciting rewards several times each day. This is the key to its amazing success.

Start the day by getting up a half-hour earlier than usual and take a walk or jog for a mile or two. If you're really serious about losing weight, you must have the self-discipline to get up early and develop the habit of exercise. Keep active and the pounds will melt like ice cream in July.

This is also the only time of the day when you can control your activities without interference. Studies have shown that about 75 percent of persons who start their exercise in the morning will continue after twelve months. About 80 percent of those who start exercising in the evening have dropped out long before twelve months pass.

While walking or running, you can imagine that about twenty feet in front of you is a beautiful (or handsome) young person of the opposite sex, and that you are determined to catch up with that person. Of course, you never do, but this adds some humor and incentive to keep up the pace. (You can substitute a MoonPie in your mind for that person, if this gives you more desire.)

After returning home, eat a good breakfast complete with milk or juice, a MoonPie, and a high-fiber cereal. For a really different and jazzy breakfast, throw milk, cereal, and a MoonPie in a blender for several minutes. This is sure to start your day off in a new and exciting manner.

At lunchtime, walk for at least thirty minutes and then enjoy a MoonPie, some fruit, and a low-calorie beverage.

For dinner ("supper" in the South), eat exactly half of the food you would normally eat (taking care to reduce the number of fatty foods in your diet). This plan does not disrupt food preparation for others in your family and lets you eat the things you enjoy.

Finally, it's important to drink lots of water all day long. The more water you drink, the better.

If you followed the diet faithfully all day, then enjoy an evening snack of your favorite MoonPie. After a few weeks, add another MoonPie for a midmorning snack.

The MoonPie can also help those who need to gain weight (if indeed such people exist). It can be the foundation of many truly fattening creations. Here are some ideas to really pile on the calories.

The Island Delight—A chocolate MoonPie floating in a bowl of molasses

The Honey Bun—A vanilla MoonPie covered with a cup of pure honey

Eskimo Divinity—Two MoonPies buried in a quart of ice cream

In 2003, deep-fried MoonPies were sold at the North Carolina State Fair and elsewhere.

No matter how or when you eat a MoonPie, it will be a treat beyond compare. You can stack them up, take them with you, and let the kids decorate them with tube-frosting drawings of flowers or their names. There's just no limit to the fun.

MoonPies and Survival

A prudent person should carry at least two dozen MoonPies in the passenger compartment of his/her car in the wintertime in cold climates. If the car is stuck in ice or snow for a long time, MoonPies make excellent survival rations. A fresh supply

NEW ON THE MENU AT N.C. STATE FAIR

MARK JOHNSON – STAFF PHOTO

State fair-goers can buy two MoonPies fried in funnel cake-like batter and covered with sugar, on a stick, for $3.

DEEP-FRIED MOONPIES

should be put in the car every two weeks or so. Use the small insulated chests, designed for holding one or two six-packs of beverages, to keep the MoonPies at a suitable temperature.

A Mr. Dwarde J. Farquhuar wrote us from Bangor, Maine about a mishap that occurred to him one winter. After he picked up a month's supply of MoonPies for his large family, his small car plunged off an icy road and landed in a huge snowdrift that completely buried the car. He was unable to get out of the car and survived on MoonPies and melted snow for seven days until he was finally rescued.

MoonPies are excellent additions to the food supply in emergency shelters but should be replaced monthly. MoonPies could make the difference between sanity and going berserk if one is confined to a shelter for a long time and forced to eat only C rations and other obnoxious canned foods.

CHAPTER 9

Entertaining MoonPie Style

So little time—so much to celebrate! We all find special moments to mark along life's passage. Sharing them with family and friends makes them even better. In this chapter, we explore some of the possibilities and times to share a special moment and a MoonPie with those we love.

MoonPies can be used to enhance parties of every kind, for both children and adults. Since the enjoyment of MoonPies knows no season, the following guide offers some suggestions for celebrating festive occasions by the month—a sort of MoonPie calendar to ensure that you haven't overlooked opportunities to rejoice with the MoonPie.

MoonPies by the Month

January

New Year's Day: MoonPies are the perfect accompaniment for black-eyed peas and turnip greens. In the South, black-eyed peas traditionally represent good luck, greens stand for wealth, and MoonPies symbolize the hope for peace and love in the New Year.

Rosh Hashanah (the Jewish New Year): It is becoming very popular to eat MoonPies dipped in a bowl of honey during Rosh Hashanah to ensure a sweet year for the faithful. The faithful have found that this is much more enjoyable than the traditional slice of apple or the customary bread, the challah, dipped in honey.

Football: MoonPies are a great dessert when tailgating at football games or while watching the big game with friends at home on television. They require no preparation and they'll fill up a hungry crowd without creating a huge mess.

February

Groundhog Day: A breakfast of hot chocolate and a MoonPie is in order as you wait for Punxsutawney Phil to emerge from his home with his annual weather report. The MoonPie can be used as bait to lure that little sucker out of his hole. MoonPies are also welcomed by the throngs of newspaper and television reporters who have been waiting all day for Punxsutawney Phil to show his face.

Valentine's Day: Trim the edges of a MoonPie with a sharp

knife to create a perfect heart shape. What could be a more loving gift for that special someone? A box of MoonPies tied with an elegant red ribbon is a gift that will show your sweetheart the depth and sincerity of your love.

March

St. Patrick's Day: For many people, this is an important celebration. Serve a platter of Mini Chocolate and Vanilla MoonPies, unwrapped and decorated with green icing shamrocks. This dessert tops off a traditional meal of corned beef and cabbage.

April

Easter: MoonPies in assorted flavors and colors make great basket stuffers for young and old alike. If you organize an egg hunt for the children, hide a few MoonPies in the yard along with the eggs to add a real surprise to the hunt. As an alternative, hide only MoonPies in the yard for a real old-fashioned Easter MoonPie Hunt. This certainly is a lot easier than fooling with eggs, especially when you step on one several weeks after the hunt.

May

Mother's Day: Instead of giving Mom a dozen roses that will soon wilt, give her a lasting gift of love for Mother's Day—a case of MoonPies. The long shelf life of MoonPies will reflect your love well into July, although the odds are that your mom will finish off the case within two weeks.

Memorial Day: Remember our veterans and also those dedicated workers at the Bakery, who have devoted their lives to making the finest marshmallow sandwich for mankind. On Memorial Day, it is perfectly appropriate to leave a half-finished MoonPie at the Tomb of the Unknown Soldier, representing a mission cut short on behalf of all of us.

(Note that this is the only exception to leaving an unfinished MoonPie unattended.)

June

Father's Day: Most Dads have enough ties, colognes, socks, and wallets. Give Dad a break and give him something he can enjoy while he relaxes on his special day—a case of MoonPies.

July

Independence Day: Holiday picnics and cookouts should be fun for everyone, including the cook! Stack up some unwrapped MoonPies and top them off with lots of small paper flags on toothpicks (sold with cake decorating supplies) to make a simple and fun dessert. Should your picnic be bothered by flies, it is permissible to take one MoonPie and place it approximately one hundred feet from your picnic site. Every fly within a quarter-mile radius will flock to this decoy noble snack, leaving you to enjoy yours without competition.

August

Vacation Time: MoonPies travel well; tuck some on top of the ice in a cooler and hit the open road. If you should get lost or encounter a long stretch of highway with no services, they will come in handy. At home, you can create a perfect summer treat by inserting a craft stick into a MoonPie and freezing it. Finally, when the Dog Days hit, turn on the oscillating fan, stretch out in a hammock and console yourself with MoonPies. Little chewing is required at these times; the MoonPies generally will soften and slide down your throat with ease.

September

Labor Day: This is another great time to enjoy your favorite snack. It's football season again—time to fill your flask and your MoonPie carrying case and head for the stands. Although it's not on the officially approved beverage list, bourbon is a very effective chaser for MoonPies. After several chasers, the Pies will go down so easily you'll think you're in the Dog Days again.

School Days: It's finally time to send the youngsters back to their classrooms. Lucky children will find a Mini MoonPie tucked into their sack lunches. A Mini MoonPie is also appreciated along with a piece of fruit or a handful of raw veggies for an after-school snack.

October

Columbus Day: Columbus sought and found the land where the MoonPie was destined to be created. Without this brave explorer, the appearance of MoonPies would have been delayed for many years.

Halloween: If you enjoy giving treats to neighborhood children, try handing out Mini MoonPies instead of candy; your house will be the most popular one on the block. To create an unusual costume for your little one, use glue or tape to attach a strip of white material around the inside edges of two large cardboard circles (painted dark brown). Leave the bottom open for the legs, and cut a hole at the top of the material to slip over the little one's head. Make two holes for the arms in the front cardboard circle and attach a logo cut from a box of MoonPies. Your little MoonPie is ready to go!

November

Veterans Day: Buy a poppy and give the veteran a MoonPie.
Thanksgiving: Not everyone loves the traditional pumpkin pie dessert. Why not offer your family and friends an alternative dessert after the Thanksgiving feast—the original MoonPie?

December

Christmas: MoonPies make excellent stocking stuffers for the children, and assorted boxes can be wrapped and placed

under the tree. Some folks have even hung MoonPies on the tree for decoration, but the pies seem to disappear if there are small children, mice, or other vermin about. An assortment of MoonPies is something that everyone will appreciate—all those people you want to remember at the holidays but just can't figure out what they'd like. Also, keep several dozen MoonPies on hand, along with plenty of hot chocolate, to give to neighborhood carolers.

Hanukkah: Because Hanukkah celebrates the miracle of oil, it is becoming a popular holiday tradition to eat deep-fried MoonPies served on popsicle sticks. This is much easier than frying pancakes made out of potatoes and onions, or jelly-filled donuts.

New Year's Eve: Ring in the New Year with a champagne toast and a MoonPie.

Other Important Events

MoonPies will come in handy at any event. At a birthday party or wedding or baby shower, they can even be used as a centerpiece. Buy a large silk bouquet and place it in a weighted flowerpot. Remove some of the large blooms and replace them with wrapped Mini MoonPies taped or hot glued securely to the stems.

The height of elegance is a wedding cake made of vanilla MoonPies, with the white pies indicating purity. In fact, your elegance can be as high as you like, since MoonPies stack wonderfully. (Note: If the happy couple has been living together prior to finally getting married, banana or chocolate MoonPies might be more appropriate.) This will make the event something that your guests will never forget. When the author's daughter was married, vanilla MoonPies, cut into quarters, graced a silver platter. The guests were thrilled to get such a special treat.

Two or three boxes sent along with the wedding couple will ensure the success of the honeymoon. Some couples never leave their honeymoon suite until their supplies of MoonPies (and perhaps they also) are exhausted.

Upon the birth of a child, instead of passing out cigars, try passing out MoonPies. (You never heard of a non-MoonPie section in a restaurant, did you?) Tie a pink ribbon around the pie for a girl or a blue ribbon for a boy. If it's twins, either a Double Decker or two singles tied together with ribbon would be suitable.

These are just a few ideas for celebrating with the MoonPie. Use your own imagination and creativity, and you'll come up with many more. We think you'll find that the MoonPie is much more than a mere snack—it's a versatile comfort food.

CHAPTER 10

MoonPie-in-the-Sky Plans

The purpose of the MoonPie Cultural Club remains the same as when it was founded. We want to share our love of the MoonPie (and our MoonPies) with everyone we meet. For those who wish to become involved in the MoonPie movement, the following charter is a good place to start. When friends band together to share MoonPies and their personal MoonPie experiences, they can request membership in the official club. To become a member chapter, send a self-addressed 10"x13" envelope, with two first-class stamps affixed, to this book's publisher and you'll soon receive an official charter.

A copy of the original charter is below.

OFFICIAL CHARTER

THE MOONPIE® CULTURAL CLUB

The _____
Chapter of the MoonPie® Cultural Club has been established and sanctioned to spread the Enjoyment, History, Vast Folklore, and Honorable Traditions of that Noble Snack, the Original MoonPie®, throughout the world.

All members of the Cub will extend the Courtesy and Hospitality always expected of persons of Honor and High Moral Character to visiting Members and will uphold those Noble Ideals and Rules of Etiquette as explained in our inspired guide, *The Great MoonPie® Handbook*.

This is the_____day of _____ , 20 ____

By the hand and Seal of _____   _____
                              President   Director of the
                                                  Chapter upon
                                                  its Founding

---

"Moon Pie®" and "MoonPie®" are registered in the U.S. Patent and Trademark Office by the Chattanooga Bakery, Inc., producers of the MoonPie.

Club members are expected to devote themselves to the cultural enlightenment of their communities and of the farthest corners of the civilized world. Suggested titles for officers include "ambassador," "diplomat," and "foreign minister."

Below is a typical letter from a director of a new chapter. This honor was obviously the highest point in his career. Note that the letter displays the proper respect and feeling of awe.

Mr. Ron Dickson Executive Director
World Headquarters
The MoonPie Cultural Club

Suite 172.5
2101-W Rexford Rd
Charlotte NC 28211 USA

Subject: Establishment of the Matthews NC Chapter of "The MoonPie Cultural Club"

Your Eminence:
It is with humility and reverence that I accept the awesome responsibility bestowed upon this unworthy servant, namely, "Director of the Matthews NC Chapter of the MoonPie Cultural Club." I hereby promise and covenant to faithfully fulfill and exercise the requirements as set forth in the "Official Charter."

Your obedient servant,
(signature)
Mac Johnston

Enclosure: Countersigned copy of the Official Charter, to be stored eternally in the Archives of the Club

The World Headquarters (WHQ) of the Cultural Club is now temporarily located in a modest building on Lake Norman, near Charlotte, North Carolina, while awaiting construction of permanent quarters. The enthusiastic and dedicated staff, entirely voluntary and unpaid, corresponds with clubs around the world. She also collects, organizes, and files information about the MoonPie.

A project in the 1980s at WHQ was the production of a beautiful color-slide presentation entitled "The Lore of the MoonPie." The narration of this exciting and humorous show was recorded in London, with background music by the Vienna Philharmonic Orchestra. The staff is busy translating the show into other civilized languages. Copies of this elegant show are in great demand for meetings of clubs and civic groups such as the Sierra Club, Kiwanis, Lions, Elks, Moose, Ex-Cons, and other organizations desirous of improving their knowledge of culture and etiquette.

A group of television engineers is preparing to transfer the slide show to DVD, in many languages, for worldwide distribution.

Members of a select group of enthusiasts called the MoonPie Patrol (MPs) diligently read newspapers and magazines from all over the world, watching for correct and incorrect references to MoonPies. They send letters of commendation to writers who recognize and praise the true MoonPie in their obviously superior articles. They send letters with correct information to writers who confuse the names "Moon Pie" and "MoonPie" with just any type of marshmallow sandwich, reminding them that "Moon Pie" and "MoonPie" are registered names and may be used only to refer to the quality products of the Chattanooga Bakery, Inc.

MPs also checks menus in the finer restaurants that offer MoonPies to be sure that the registration symbol (®) is printed there and that the marshmallow sandwich being sold is the genuine item, not some cheap imitation.

Many dedicated MPs also monitor television and radio broadcasts to ensure that speakers refer to MoonPies correctly.

MPs are authorized to wear gold lapel pins to signify their coveted membership in this elite group.

Caps

MoonPie baseball caps come in several distinctive colors suitable for various occasions. Some uses are suggested below.

White is for church on Sunday, if you have behaved during the previous week

Light blue is for golf and other outdoor sports

Tan is for fishing

Dark blue is worn in bars and at business meetings

Black is for funerals and shotgun weddings of close relatives

Fancy black is for Mardi Gras

Red and white is for dining in fancy restaurants, such as barbecue lodges. It is highly recommended when dating hot chicks and breathless babes.

The sun visor is for ladies with fancy hairstyles

And finally, for former vice president Dick Cheney's hunting buddies, there is now blaze orange. (While on a hunting trip, Cheney accidentally shot one of his buddies with buckshot. The victim recovered with only minor damage.)
And if you wear this orange cap while escorting a fetching, frisky, and fabulous filly, it tells your buddies to back off—this is my *girl!*

The Official T-Shirt

The official MoonPie T-shirt is available on the Bakery's Website. The large logo is printed on the front and back, in color, on a light blue or tan T-shirt made in America. The size of the logo is adjusted according to the size of the garment. This collector's item will create a sensation at the office, picnics, or wherever you dare to be seen in it.

The author frequently had to meet strangers at the airport. For positive identification, he wore his MoonPie T-shirt, with the big logo on the front and back. As one stranger said, "I could see you coming and going from a great distance."

If a golfer wearing a MoonPie T-shirt passes out from too much sunshine (or moonshine), his friends can identify him whether he is lying face up or down.

Ladies' nightshirts have a small MoonPie logo printed high on the left chest, above the curve of the bosom.

T-shirts printed front and back (note that the one on the right has the old-fashioned logo)

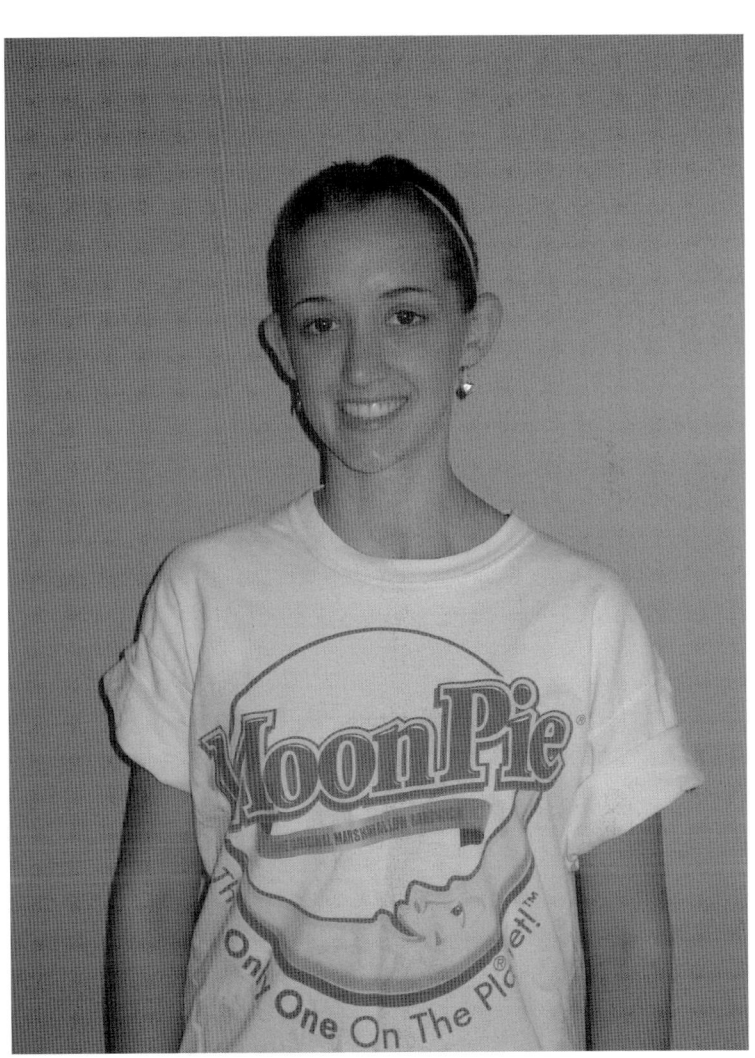

Official MoonPie polo shirt (photographs courtesy of Molly Chase, Troy, New York)

Personal Accessories

A team of internationally famous designers and craftsmen is working on a collection of windbreakers, iron-on patches, ties, tie clasps, jewelry, belt buckles, decals, mugs, ashtrays, towels, and blankets. Earmuffs with the official logo would be a snazzy item for cold days. These items should be available before next winter.

One creative fan of the MoonPie, Lynda Stinson Hollar, made a MoonPie pillow to add a touch of elegance to her living room.

Some inspired interior designers use leftover MoonPie wrappers to make wallpaper and also borders on office walls next to the ceiling or around the upper part of cubicles. This shows all visitors that the occupant is a dedicated fan of the MoonPie.

The MoonPie Emblem for Business Attire

An embroidered MoonPie logo is available for subtle display *inside* the pocket on a man's white dress shirt. (The cloth logo is stapled to a white index card in order to keep the logo properly aligned.) In this manner, MoonPie boosters in the business world can discretely recognize each other and share the bond of universal friendship in an unobtrusive way. (Well-endowed ladies should refrain from carrying the logo with this method for obvious reasons.)

Tags for Cars

A tag with the MoonPie logo is available for the front bumper of your car, if you live in a state that issues only one tag. You can also display this tag in the rear window of your pickup or car to help you find your vehicle in the Walmart parking lot.

Some devoted fans have ordered custom license plates for their cars that spell out "MOONPIE," "MOONPIES," "MOONPIE2," and so forth. They willingly pay the extra fee, often twenty or thirty dollars, to their state governments for this rare privilege.

Bumper Stickers

A number of phrases are available on bumper stickers, in cartons of twenty-five:

>MoonPies—A Way of Life
>Seven Days Without a MoonPie Makes One Weak
>Go for It—a MoonPie!
>I'd Rather Be Eating a MoonPie
>Honk if You Crave a MoonPie
>MoonPie Eaters Do It with a Smile on Their Faces
>Have You Hugged Your MoonPie Today?

MoonPie Hardhat

Many construction site foremen glue the MoonPie logo from a wrapper on the front of their hardhats to make themselves easily identifiable to new workers and visitors. To inspire the workers, some enlightened foremen distribute MoonPies for their Thursday morning break.

Foreign Language Translations

Work has begun to translate this book into most of the civilized languages, such as Arabic, German, French, Spanish, Portuguese, Norwegian, Swedish, Greek, Turkish, and Afrikaans.

MoonPie Compact Discs (CDs) and DVDs

The complete text of *The Great MoonPie® Handbook* will soon be available on compact discs (CDs). This exciting recording is an excellent gift for busy executives who need to refresh their memories on the history and culture of the noble snack, for the illiterate, and for the blind. The narration is by a cultured British lady whose accent can be clearly understood by the entire English-speaking world. The Vienna Philharmonic Orchestra provides background music. For a gift that a loved one will never forget, send a box of fresh MoonPies along with the CDs.

There soon will be regional and ethnic versions of the CDs, recorded by famous persons who are eager to add this performance to their lists of major accomplishments. We expect to give the narrators complete freedom to express the basic themes of the book in their own words. (We do reserve the right to censor.)

Posters for Your Home or Office

Posters are available with several slogans, including:

> MoonPies are a way of life.
> MoonPies are a part of living.
> Enjoy a MoonPie with a friend.
> You deserve the best—enjoy a MoonPie tonight.
> A week without a MoonPie is like a week without . . .
> He won't be happy until he gets it. A MoonPie.
> I'd walk a mile for a MoonPie.
> A MoonPie in every lunch bag.
> Enjoy the originals: Coca-Cola and a MoonPie.
> We will sell no MoonPie after its time.
> MoonPie—good to the last bite.

Ideas for Parties and Social Events

The following kits were designed to help spread the word about the original MoonPie and to encourage the proper enjoyment of them.

The Office Party Kit

This kit contains a description of this important social event, sample announcements, nametags, and colorful posters.

The Office Patio Picnic Kit

This is a complete description of a noontime social gathering on the front patio of a large office building. A MoonPie and beverage are sold at cost, and the guests bring a sandwich and so on. Nametags, in various colors to identify each company, are encouraged to help people meet each other. The list of equipment needed mentions picnic tables with benches, small tables and chairs, lawn chairs, iceboxes, umbrellas to shade the MoonPies, invitations, and a sample guest list of local, state, and national dignitaries. Sample announcements, RSVP forms for employees, bug repellent, colorful posters, and a clever "ice calculator" complete the kit.

Patio picnics are held in the spring and fall so that single people can meet each other without the burdens of concealing winter coats or the discomforts of oppressive summer heat.

The MoonPie Festival Week Kit for Colleges

Based on a real event at East Carolina University in North Carolina, this magnificent kit contains sample banners (3'x5'); posters; sample printed invitations for such notables as the president of the United States, Queen Elizabeth of England, and Elizabeth Taylor; and a description of contests and sporting events involving MoonPies. The objective is to create a lifelong impression of the noble snack in the fertile minds of students who participate in this festive and cultural event.

The College Exam Survival Kit

The MoonPie exam kit is designed to help a college student survive the rigors of studying for final exams. It supplies almost all the required nutrients for a seven-day period. The kit contains:

24 MoonPies, assorted flavors
2 boxes raisins
12 granola bars
9 chocolate bars
5 bags peanuts
2 boxes bran cereal
7 cans orange juice
7 apples, fresh
1 jar instant coffee
1 box sugar cubes
1 jar creamer
14 cans soup, assorted
1 lb. cheese
1 box crackers
1 toothbrush
1 tube toothpaste
1 bottle aspirin

High School MoonPie Clubs

MoonPie clubs have been organized spontaneously in high schools all over the country. One of the most famous was at Olympic High School in Charlotte, North Carolina during the 1970s. Through their own efforts, primitive as they were, dozens of students (some of whom were also primitive) organized, had T-shirts printed, devised a secret sign of recognition and a greeting, and chartered a bus to the home of the MoonPie.

The MoonPie Connoisseurs' Convention

The annual convention is held in Chattanooga in the spring. The highlight of the meeting is the banquet, where all past and presently produced flavors of the MoonPie are available. All of the gourmet desserts are prepared by the best chefs in the land.

Seminars cover a broad range of subjects, such as "Detecting Counterfeit MoonPies," "Writing Letters to Get MoonPies into

Your Favorite Stores and Restaurants," "Teaching the Culture of MoonPies to Immigrants," etc. Films are presented on the etiquette of serving and eating MoonPies. Shops sell the latest attire associated with the MoonPie.

For active types, golf and tennis championships, shuffleboard, and MoonPie Flying Saucer contests are offered. (These are Frisbees with the MoonPie logo on both sides.) Each champion wins a year's supply of MoonPies.

Moonlight Madness MoonPie Festival

Each year in the autumn, there is a festival in Chattanooga for true devotees. It is held after dark in the parking lot in front of the Bakery and is timed to coincide with the rising of the harvest moon over the esteemed building. There are charter flights of Boeing 747 jets, each with the MoonPie logo emblazoned on the tail, from major cities in the land to Chattanooga. Overflow traffic and private planes are diverted to nearby Swan Creek International Airport and Pasture. (Pilots are advised to buzz the field at least once to scare the cows out of the way.)

The Chattanooga mayor, governor of Tennessee, and officials of the Bakery present toasts and speeches extolling the noble confection. Contests, a craft fair, and concert bring throngs of MoonPie fans. "The Lore of the MoonPie" and film tributes are shown.

Fall is a beautiful time of year in east Tennessee, and millions of tourists already visit the nearby Smoky Mountains to see the colorful fall leaves. This festival is a time for all MoonPie pilgrims to pay homage to and share the culture and folklore of this delicious snack.

The Grand Excursion to the MoonPie Bakery and Tour of the Area

This popular pilgrimage takes you on a visit to the Bakery and includes samples of the fresh product and a copious supply of RC Cola. Also included on this memorable tour are a side trip to Lookout Mountain, a ride on the Chattanooga Choo-Choo train, and the Autumn Leaf Tour (in season, of course). This can be the greatest experience of your life, comparable to visiting Mecca, Rome, Paris, or London. Gift certificates are available for your loved ones, or for your family.

The MoonPie Cultural College

A college has been established as the official repository of the culture, vast folklore, history, and honorable traditions associated with the noble snack, and to impart this knowledge and some degree of refinement to deserving students. It shares the campus of a prestigious university in Charlotte, North Carolina, recognized for its rich heritage. This joint venture has added new enthusiasm, fame, and money (of course) to this esteemed institution.

The vast MoonPie Library includes all the newspaper articles, magazine stories, and books ever written about the MoonPie. There is also an unusual oral-history collection of stories told by retired salesmen and other employees of the Bakery. The library was also fortunate to receive originals and copies of home movies taken by employees since 1917. The other side of this room displays MoonPie advertisements dating back to 1917. It is indeed a treasure house of priceless knowledge.

Another building on the lovely campus is home to the MoonPie Museum. This contains the first four-and-a-half-inch cookie cutter, some of the baking equipment used to produce the first pies, wrappers and cartons covering the entire history of the product, original advertising posters, pictures of famous salesmen, and other priceless artifacts. One of the most unusual exhibits is a box of MoonPies recovered recently from the cache of provisions left in Alaska in 1925 by a team racing to the North Pole by dogsled. This is on permanent display in a glass case refrigerated to zero degrees Fahrenheit.

Students of the college are expected to learn MoonPie history and etiquette during the first semester, then pass on (or out) to mastering the beverage guide. Typical classes include

Distinguishing Between Real and Imitation MoonPies, Preparation of Gourmet Desserts, Promotion of Social Events to Honor the MoonPie, and The Sociological Influence (if Any) of MoonPies upon the Inhabitants of the North American Continent. *The Great MoonPie® Handbook* serves as the outline for this intensive curriculum. Upon graduation, students are awarded the degree of Doctor of MoonPie Culture, a case of pies, and a copy of the *Handbook,* numbered and signed by the president of the college.

Visitors to the campus will be inspired to see such spotless grounds and happy students enthusiastically discussing new ways to spread the lore of the MoonPie. It is expected, of course, that the Cultural College will become part of the Greater University of North Carolina and provide some sorely needed leadership in its area of expertise.

MoonPie Cheerleaders

MoonPie cheerleaders are being organized at Cultural Clubs all over the nation. (Rejects are sent on to the Dallas Cowboys cheerleader squad.) MoonPie cheerleaders are available to add excitement and sparkle to cultural events (or, in some cases, uncultural events).

Innovative Ideas

As the MoonPie's fame continues to spread and its distribution widens into the international market, the MoonPie Cultural Club is striving to keep pace with developments by implementing several innovative ideas. Working together with the Chattanooga Bakery, we hope to see some of these ideas turned into realities.

MoonPie Calendar

Three concepts are being explored. One is for a traditional paper calendar depicting people enjoying their favorite snack. Scenes from MoonPie folklore would be included.

A designer is also working on the concept of a round calendar. The MoonPie logo will be very inconspicuous. A faint background color on each page will hint at the colors of different MoonPie flavors. Many scenes of MoonPie folklore will make the calendar a treasured keepsake for many years. We confidently predict that this calendar will achieve the same status as great works of art by Norman Rockwell, Currier and Ives, and Ansel Adams.

The third calendar would be much more short-lived, since

it calls for edible pages. At the end of each month, you would simply remove the chocolate-covered cookie on which the days had been printed and eat it. To ensure freshness, this calendar would be issued quarterly.

Poetry Contest

Club members would also like to see the Bakery use its Web site to hold an annual poetry contest open to fans around the world. Excluding professional writers, the contest would allow people from all walks of life to share their MoonPie poems with others.

A world-famous poet, Mr. Vladimir Jones, is researching the history, folklore, traditions, customs, and fantasies of the MoonPie. His "Ode to a Chattanooga MoonPie" is expected to surpass the popularity of the poems by Robert Louis Stevenson. If Stevenson could write such great poetry while inspired only by tea and crumpets, imagine what our poet will create while motivated by the incredible MoonPie.

Official Recognition by States and Nations

A campaign is under way to have the MoonPie declared the official snack of all states and countries where it is sold. This will be a fitting tribute to the snack that helped to build a nation, as millions of workers will be glad to testify. The lead-off state in America, of course, will be Tennessee.

Anthem

The official MoonPie song will be completed soon and will add a joyous sound to all MoonPie events. The composer will use a full orchestra to produce the majestic sound appropriate for the theme. A brass section of twelve trumpets and a real cannon would create the proper volume.

A special version will be written for the harmonica, ukulele, or guitar so that the anthem may be played anywhere.

MoonPie Rest Stops on Interstate Highways

According to Ralph W. Grigg, Esq., a campaign is now under way to have the MoonPie logo attached to some rest-stop signs on interstate highways. This will tell the motoring public, at least those with discriminating taste, that at the next rest stop, fresh MoonPies will be in the vending machines. The logo, of course, will be small and in good taste and not at all gaudy. This small gesture will add immensely to the pleasure of driving.

The MoonPie Research Foundation

The foundation will offer scholarships and grants to students who are willing to dedicate their lives to researching the influence of MoonPies upon the culture and lives of inhabitants of the North American continent. Required traits in the recipients are the ability to write in a humorous style, a devotion to sociological research, and a stomach strong enough for a diet of fried chicken, country ham, mashed potatoes, and green peas.

The MoonPie of the Month Club (Coming Soon, We Hope)

The MoonPie of the Month Club would be a special service for people who find it difficult to buy MoonPies at their regular grocery store. After joining the club, you would receive shipments of your favorite MoonPies each month at your home or office. Although the usual interval between shipments would be four weeks, shorter or longer periods could be specified. Advance payment would be accepted quarterly and placed in an escrow account until a shipment is made. A sophisticated computer system would automatically prepare shipping labels and invoices when appropriate. The prepayment plan would enable customers to enjoy discounted costs and would eliminate the expense and inconvenience of C.O.D. shipments.

The following assortments of MoonPies would be shipped to you monthly by private carrier. Although not available through retail outlets, special selections of single decker MoonPies (by the case) could be ordered through the MoonPie Cultural Club's World Headquarters.

The Senator: 8 dozen chocolate
The Delta Queen: 8 dozen vanilla
The Juan Valdez: 8 dozen banana
The Watusi Chieftain: 8 dozen lemon
The Executive: 4 dozen vanilla, 2 dozen chocolate, 2 dozen banana
The Ambassador: 2 dozen chocolate, 2 dozen vanilla, 2 dozen lemon, 2 dozen banana
The Captain: 3 dozen chocolate, 3 dozen banana, 1 dozen vanilla, 1 dozen lemon
The Slam Dunk: 7 dozen chocolate, 1 dozen vanilla
The Whiteman Sampler: 4 dozen vanilla, 2 dozen lemon, 2 dozen banana

We regret that the Bakery does not have the facilities at this time to operate the MoonPie of the Month Club. Every square foot of the Bakery is needed now just to produce MoonPies.

Gourmet Flavors

An intensive research project is under way to develop some or all of the following flavors of MoonPies: cherry, chocolate chip, coffee, maple, and crunch (with puffed rice). This project involves food scientists, nutritionists, chemists, packaging experts, buyers of ingredients, accountants, the Bakery's shipping department, marketing consultants, and five small, hungry children who have final approval of new flavors. When they first become available, the gourmet flavors will be distributed only to members of the MoonPie of the Month Club.

Official Suppliers to the Cultural Club, by Appointment

After resisting an overwhelming demand for many years, the club has agreed to designate certain firms as "Official Suppliers to the MoonPie Cultural Club." An appropriate crest and shield, surpassing the artistic merit of the British design ("By Royal Appointment to the Crown"), is being created. Many suppliers have felt that the MoonPie crest would be worth thousands of dollars in advertising and would help their businesses to grow and prosper. Millions of people trust the MoonPie and would expect guaranteed quality in any item bearing the crest. This is indeed an awesome responsibility.

CHAPTER 11

The Impact of MoonPies Upon the World

When the history of the world is finally written, there can be little doubt that a major chapter will be devoted to the impact of MoonPies upon modern man. Even now, scholars continue to study the wide-ranging political, social, and cultural effects that this unpretentious product from Tennessee has had upon civilization. This chapter will explore certain dramatic cases.

Huey "Kingpie" Short

Perhaps the best example of how MoonPies have influenced politics can be seen in the life and career of the Southern politician Huey "Kingpie" Short. Born the son of an itinerant encyclopedia salesman from Gulfstream, Alabama, Huey was raised on a steady diet of encyclopedias and MoonPies. By the time Huey turned thirteen, he had read the *Encyclopaedia Britannica* seven times and, by his own estimate, had consumed 11,284 MoonPies. Shortly after his fourteenth birthday, he quit school to "spread the good word 'bout MoonPies and sell those books."[1]

In 1936, Huey retired from the encyclopedia business a wealthy man. At the age of thirty-three he was considered by many to be the most successful salesman in the South.

Upon retiring, Short turned his full attention toward promoting MoonPies. When World War II broke out, he saw the conflict as an opportunity to introduce Americans from all walks of life to his beloved passion. With this in mind, he attempted to enlist in all three branches of the armed forces but was rejected each time for medical reasons. It seems that long years of carrying suitcases full of encyclopedias caused one of his arms to grow a full four inches longer than the other. Years later Huey would confide to a friend, "Unconsciously I suppose I knew that I had become physically unbalanced. Yet my tailor never said a word."[2] Disheartened and depressed, Huey decided to enter politics, having no worthwhile career to pursue.

The Kingpie's climb to national prominence was meteoric. Rising quickly through the local levels of politics, he gained national attention in 1942 by running for the U.S. Senate. His campaign slogan, "A MoonPie in every lunch bucket," soon became part of the American political lexicon.

As a member of the Senate, Short introduced numerous bills involving MoonPies. MoonPie school lunch programs, MoonPie programs for the aged, and a national MoonPie Day all became parts of his proposed legislation. Then at the peak of his career, he was suddenly cut down by an assassin. Huey was making a speech on the steps of the Capitol when a young man stepped from the crowd wielding a chocolate MoonPie. Before the assailant could be subdued, Short had been hit full in the face by the chocolate-encrusted cookie. The press was quick to pounce upon the incident, referring to Short as "that marshmallow politician."[3] Physically unharmed, Short was nevertheless a broken man. His spirit destroyed, he eventually was forced to give up his seat in the Senate and subsequently faded from the political scene. Ironically, the very product that he worked so hard to promote had played a direct role in his downfall.

Today, historians continue the debate over Huey Short's exact place in the annals of American politics. Still, no one can deny the impact he had upon America's conscience. As one historian recently pointed out, "He may not have gotten any legislation passed, but no one will ever forget the Kingpie."[4]

The Pago Pago Islands

From time to time scientists ae afforded the rare opportunity to study a social group or community under laboratory conditions. Such was the case in 1962 when a band of scientists discovered an isolated tribe living on a remote island of the Pago Pago chain in the Pacific Ocean. An aerial survey of the island had revealed a large, apparently manmade structure resembling a MoonPie. Upon actual examination, the structure turned out to be exactly as it first appeared: a forty-foot model of a MoonPie made entirely of bamboo. Scientists were at first puzzled over this amazing discovery. Then, slowly, the story of the Cow Cow Hoetek tribe began to unfold.

It seems that one night in 1944 the tribe was awakened by an aircraft circling very low over the island. A short time later they heard a loud explosion and saw a flash of light emanating from the island's south shore.

The next morning the tribe went to investigate the source of the disturbance and discovered the tail of a large plane. In addition, scattered along the beach were hundreds of boxes containing individually wrapped marshmallow confections. At first the natives were interested only in the tail section protruding from the edge of the water. Soon, however, someone opened one of the packages and bit into the contents. Then all hell broke loose. Within minutes tribesmen had gathered up all the boxes on the beach and began to transport them back to their huts. Each tribesman established a cache of his own and soon after this event both the social structure and cultural fabric of the tribe began to change rapidly.

In his groundbreaking work, *The Cow Cow and the MoonPie*, Dr. Eric L. Crotchlow details the rapid transformation of the Hoeteks. In the book's introduction Dr. Crotchlow wrote, "Who could imagine the effect this dandy little Southern treat would have upon an entire people?"[5] The changes were indeed dramatic. Standards and traditions that had survived thousands of years were suddenly discarded overnight. Most notably, the Hoetek barter system was completely rearranged around the MoonPie.

Traditionally, Hoetek men had traded goats for wives. Before the arrival of the MoonPies, three goats would almost always assure the acquisition of a chieftain's daughter. A week later, however, up to five women at a time were being traded for a single box of MoonPies. Moreover, as the supply of MoonPies began to dwindle, the price began to escalate rapidly until a dozen goats and twenty-three women became the going rate for a single MoonPie. "How extraordinary," Dr. Crotchlow noted, "for anyone to equate goats with MoonPies."[6]

The rest of the Hoetek story is a sad tale of avarice and dissention. As the supply of MoonPies continued to dwindle, bloodshed became inevitable. One tribesman, insanely jealous over another's cache, would dispatch his neighbor and eat the booty. The women, on the other hand, having been totally discarded, eventually left the island to find a more meaningful existence. Sometime around 1958, the very last MoonPie was eaten and shortly thereafter the giant replica was erected by the few remaining men. According to Dr. Crotchlow, the monument was built "in hopes of once again luring that divine hand that had originally dumped its gift upon the Hoetek."[7]

Notes
(Provided by William M. Clark)

1. J. H. Abbot, *Kingpie: The Huey Short Story* (Chicago: Rooster Books, 1968), 52.
2. E. J. Condon, *The MoonPie Monarch* (New York: Puttering Press, 1966), 183.
3. H. P. Fulton, "Marshmallow Politics," *The Free American*, sec. 2, August 12, 1943, 1.
4. Ibid., 982.
5. Eric L. Crotchlow, *The Cow Cow and the MoonPie* (Philadelphia: Explorer Press, 1965), 32.
6. Ibid., 57.
7. Ibid., 176.

Inspired Celebrations

After the *Handbook* was first published, artists across the land began painting pictures that included the MoonPie. A popular subject was an old barn whose side was covered with advertising signs for Lucky Strike, Purina, Coca-Cola, and "MoonPie."

Painting by Clinton R. Dean

The Space Program and MoonPies

In the 1960s, the National Aeronautics and Space Administration (NASA) requested that the Bakery develop a crumb-free Moon Pie for the astronauts making the first trip to the moon. NASA felt that the symbolism would help publicize this first voyage to another planetary body. The Bakery declined to adulterate their noble product in any way, suggesting instead that NASA hire astronauts with bigger mouths, large enough to eat the four-inch MoonPie in one gulp. The Bakery later agreed, however, to make a special run of bite-sized MoonPies for the next lunar landing. An extra-thick chocolate coating would prevent crumbs from floating around the spaceship and damaging electronic equipment.

In 1984, the Bakery announced the "Delta" mini double

decker, which was three and three-eighths inches in diameter. It could be eaten in one bite (or gulp) by most men, thus solving the problem of crumbs in space flights. Was this the answer to NASA's request? The Bakery, declining to exploit an association with the space program, replied, "No comment." After a few years of low sales, the Delta size was dropped.

In 1998, the Bakery began producing a new Mini MoonPie, about two and seven-tenths inches in diameter. It was perfect for space travel. In North Carolina, many highway patrolmen favor this bite-sized snack because the whole thing goes in their mouths, thus avoiding crumbs on their shirts while cruising down the highway at eighty miles per hour.

In 2003, the U.S. Department of Defense ordered 45,000 cases of single decker MoonPies for the troops in Iraq. The Bakery wisely put a thicker chocolate coating on the pies to prevent damage from the desert heat. The snacks were trucked to Norfolk, Virginia in lots of 15,000 cases. A battleship and an aircraft carrier transported the snacks as cargo to Iraq. Imagine how this taste of home must have improved the morale of our troops. CNN showed an American soldier giving a MoonPie to a smiling youngster in Baghdad.

Advertising Slogans and Popular Sayings

The millions and millions of consumers of MoonPies over the years invented many famous sayings and slogans that were originally associated with the MoonPie. Many of the advertising slogans have been changed and used for other products in desperate need of a catchy phrase. Following are some examples:

> "I'd walk a mile for a MoonPie." (. . . for a Camel.)
> "A MoonPie a day keeps the doctor away." (An apple a day . . .)
> "We will sell no MoonPie after its time." (. . . will sell no wine before its time.) (Although it should be noted that the MoonPie has an unusually long shelf life—approximately four months.)

"MoonPies are good to the last bite." (. . . to the last drop—Maxwell House coffee.)

"Love is never having to say, 'Honey, we're out of MoonPies.'"

"MoonPie—a little dab'll never do you."

"Baseball, hot dogs, MoonPies, and Chevrolet."

"Bet you can't eat just one . . . MoonPie."

"America is bullish on MoonPies."

"MoonPies taste good like a marshmallow sandwich should."

"A MoonPie is . . . a handful of love." (Uttered by Wayne Snyder on WBTV in 1982. Not yet stolen by others, who should note that it is now copyrighted.)

"I'd stop anything for a MoonPie." (To be accompanied by pictures of persons in various dangerous or pleasurable situations, stopping to enjoy a MoonPie.)

The MoonPie and the Worldwide Automobile Industry

The Man Will Never Fly Memorial Society International invited the author to give a speech at Nags Head, near Kitty Hawk, North Carolina, to explain how the MoonPie had influenced the worldwide automobile industry. He described how, after World War II, Japanese visitors toured American factories. They noticed how MoonPies and soft drinks inspired the workers to achieve greater productivity and creativity. Upon returning home, the Japanese followed this example in their automotive industry. The rest is history.

The text of the speech is in the appendix.

At the meeting, Mike Collins, an astronaut on Apollo XI,

which went to the moon, signed a MoonPie box lid and presented it to the author.

How MoonPies Saved the Charlotte Symphony Orchestra

When the Charlotte Symphony Orchestrawent on strike in 1991, the Charlotte Chapter of the MoonPie Cultural Club came to the rescue. Within several days, the musicians had free office space for a year, equipped with furniture, a copier, computer system, telephone system, and truckload of supplies.

After the strike ended, the Charlotte Chapter served refreshments to the symphony at rehearsals, featuring MoonPies and soft drinks. This is the only symphony in America that has received such support from devoted fans.

CHAPTER 12

The Man in the Moon

"Take me to your MoonPies" is likely to be the computerized greeting coming from the first extraterrestrial to land on this planet.

Recently, D. W. Smart, a MoonPie aficionado who has extensively researched the origin of the noble snack, jolted the academic world by publishing his "E.T. Theory" in the *National Enquirer*. Smart suggested that the traveling salesman who made that historic suggestion at the Chattanooga Bakery on that fateful day back in 1917 was not a salesman at all but in reality an "extraterrestrial," blessed with intelligence and culture light years in advance of our own. What if the noble snack was his civilization's highest gift to ours?

"The name *Moon*Pie was no coincidence at all," wrote Smart, "but rather a clue left for future generations. If my theory isn't so, then just explain to me why Rod Serling died while working on a television documentary entitled, *Snack Foods of the Gods.*"

Smart's theory that extraterrestrials brought MoonPies to earth could explain some quotes by famous people that have perplexed historians for years. In fact, many of these original quotes were modified because historians couldn't figure out their meanings (see chapter 6).

A Tribute to the Formerly Unknown Salesman

By the late 1950s, the MoonPie's popularity had grown so much that the Bakery lacked the resources to produce anything else. Eventually, the MoonPie became closely associated with RC Cola ® because neither product was expensive and both were filling, and a beloved Southern tradition was born. The phrase "RC Cola and a MoonPie" was so common in the region that it became a part of the fabric of the South itself.

Extraterrestrial theories aside, the MoonPie idea was Earl  Wayne Mitchell, Sr.'s enduring accomplishment—something that the snack's fans appreciate to this day. Born on April 13, 1884, in the small community of Caney Branch, Tennessee, about thirteen miles from Greenville, to David Robinson and Sarah Easterly Mitchell, he was the second of the farm couple's three sons. At an early age, he left the farm and went to Newport, Tennessee, where he found his first job. At some point, he moved to Knoxville, Tennessee, where he spent the rest of his life. This is the first known picture taken of Earl Sr.

 Earl Sr. lived in Knoxville, but he worked for the Mountain City Mill Company and the Chattanooga Bakery. On October 31, 1907, he married the love of his life, Anne Allen Bibee. In August of 1914 he was promoted to manager of the Knoxville branch of the Chattanooga Bakery, and later that same year the couple's first child, Anna Pearl, was born. In 1916, Earl Wayne "Buddy" Mitchell, Jr., came

along. This picture of the family was taken sometime in the early 1920s.

Mr. and Mrs. Earl W. Mitchell

Mrs. Mitchell was one of six children, and two of her brothers (Harry Penland Bibee and Beverly Buford Bibee) and a sister (Pearl Rose Bibee) all worked at the Bakery's Knoxville branch for a time. After Earl Sr.'s death on October 21, 1945, following a short illness, Pearl Rose was made manager of the Knoxville branch, until her death on December 1, 1947.

These two pictures of Bakery trucks were taken about 1934. Both show Earl Sr.'s nephew, Harry Penland Bibee, Jr., behind the wheel. In one picture, the words *Chattanooga Bakery, Knoxville Branch* are visible on the side of the truck. In the other picture, Harry Sr. is handing his son an early-day MoonPie.

Inventor of the MoonPie in 1917

The MoonPie's label reads, *Lookout MoonPie*. The Chattanooga Bakery was called the Lookout Bakery in those days, as it was located near Lookout Mountain, Tennessee.

Mr. Mitchell died in Knoxville. He was buried in Union Cemetery in Newport, Tennessee (near the North Carolina border). The MoonPie Cultural Club is happy that MoonPie fans everywhere can finally acknowledge the accomplishment

of Earl Wayne Mitchell, Sr.—the formerly unknown salesman.

The above plaque was added to Mr. Mitchell's gravesite in 2004 by Anna P. Pratt, the eldest grandchild of the inventor of the MoonPie.

Earl Wayne "Buddy" Mitchell, Jr., was born on December

30, 1916, in Knoxville, Tennessee. He died on July 13, 2002, in Columbia, South Carolina, and was buried there in Bush River Garden Cemetery. He is survived by his wife, Jean Alexander Mitchell, and sons, Randy "Skipper" Mitchell and Wayne Alexander Mitchell.

CHAPTER 13

The MoonPie Tradition

The Great MoonPie® Handbook had its humble beginnings in Charlotte, North Carolina. In the spring of 1981, the author found himself trying to explain the noble traditions and the enjoyment of MoonPies to some less informed employees of a large international computer company. To many of the native employees, it quickly became obvious that the workers and managers ("snowbirds") imported from other regions of this country were totally ignorant of Southern culture, gentle humor, and the MoonPie. Many of these people had grown up in culturally deprived and backward regions of this and other countries.

In a spirit of hospitality and sly amusement, the natives began teaching the newcomers the history, folklore, culture, honorable traditions, and etiquette regarding the noble snack. When facts were missing, wild imagination and creativity took over.

Having no culture of their own of which to be proud, the grateful newcomers eagerly learned the MoonPie manners and how to enjoy snacking with cultured and refined people. These newly acquired social skills enabled them to be quickly accepted by their new friends and neighbors.

Eventually these discussions became so meaningful and humorous that it seemed important to put them into writing. The result was a short pamphlet of a dozen or so pages that was distributed to those who were unfamiliar with the complexities of true Southern culture.

The idea soon seized the hearts and minds of several employees, who began to devote their lunch hours, often the most creative part of the day, to developing an expanded version of the pamphlet. The brilliance and wit of their insights were astounding and occasionally bordered on the profound. When word of the new handbook leaked out through the local press, the demand for copies became overwhelming. It was obvious that publication and national distribution were required to preserve and further spread the noble traditions of one of mankind's greatest creations—the original MoonPie.

The MoonPie Cultural Club was formed to spread the story of the MoonPie and to establish chapters throughout the civilized world. The club's devoted executive director (later designated president for life), Ron Dickson, set out to find a publisher who would make the handbook available to the general public. For several months in 1983, he collected a stack of rejection slips.

Finally, in November of 1983, Ron sent a copy of the handbook to Sam C. Rawls, the gifted cartoonist (known as Scrawls) who illustrated the book *How to Speak Southern*. Mr. Rawls, deeply moved by the handbook and inspired by a second great opportunity to bring more culture to America, drew about twenty clever cartoons over the Thanksgiving holidays. He sent them to World Headquarters of the club and, in his typically humble way, suggested that the cartoons be used in the book instead of prosaic photographs.

A partnership was formed and an intensive search for the right publisher began. Dozens of rejections were received from publishers located in the Snow Belt. It seemed that most of them had lost their sense of humor and, having no real culture of their own, they simply couldn't appreciate the noble traditions of others.

Refusing to admit defeat, Sam and Ron noted that the "ring eclipse" of May 30, 1984, resembled a chocolate MoonPie with the marshmallow oozing out all around the pie. The shadow of the eclipse passed over Columbus, Georgia (home of RC Cola), Atlanta (home of Sam and Coca-Cola), near

Chattanooga, Tennessee (home of the MoonPie), and over Charlotte (home of Ron and the MoonPie Cultural Club), and then out over the Atlantic Ocean. It completely bypassed the Snow Belt publishers. Millions of people wondered how the path of the eclipse had been arranged to pass over such significant locations. Furthermore, it all happened on Sam's birthday.

Not being at all superstitious, but believing this to be a sign from the heavens, Sam and Ron concentrated their search for a publisher located only in the path of the eclipse. Consequently, the manuscript was sent to a Georgia publisher, who decided on October 18, 1984, to publish the *Handbook* on April 1, 1985, and make it available throughout the civilized world. In the history of America, this date of publication is second in importance only to that great day when the first MoonPie was created, whatever that day might have been in 1917.

Time has brought many changes that encouraged the author to update the original manuscript. This second edition, published by the great Southern publisher, Pelican Publishing Company, Inc., continues the tradition of honoring the past, present, and future of the MoonPie. Our love of the MoonPie ties us together as a family—men and women, old and young, rich and poor. We celebrate our unity and happily continue our tradition.

Readers are encouraged to send their comments and suggestions to:

> The MoonPie Cultural Club
> 2487 Brawley School Road
> Mooresville NC 28117-7352

Complaints and unkind remarks will, as always, be ignored.

If we choose to publish any submitted material in future editions, you will receive proper credit unless you request otherwise. Letters, artwork, and manuscripts will be returned only if you include a self-addressed stamped envelope. All items submitted without a return envelope become the property of the MoonPie Cultural Club.

Appendix

Talk to the Man Will Never Fly Memorial Society

The Secret Behind the Development of the International Automobile Industry

Distinguished visitors, honored guests, and members, I will speak tonight on the history of the automobile industry. I will be reporting for the first time in public the startling secret behind the development of the worldwide automobile industry. The most significant event was not the introduction of the Model T Ford or the invention of the assembly line by Henry Ford. I also might add that the best incentive for auto workers has not been a yearly increase in wages but something else. In a few minutes I will reveal to you what has been the key to the success of this industry around the world and what has been the greatest morale booster ever created for workers.

My research took me to Japan. There, I learned that after World War II, Japanese products were known worldwide for their poor quality. In 1947, the leaders of Japanese industry sent teams of experts to America to learn the secrets of our wartime production miracles. The teams traveled thousands of miles and visited hundreds of factories. After months of diligent research, they submitted their conclusion on a single 3x5 card. I was able to obtain this original card from the Japanese Museum of Culture and Business. It says simply:

Gai ni men di eun gun eu bien. Translated into English, it says: "Give *MoonPies* to the workers!"

The Japanese leaders were astounded. "What under the Rising Sun is a MoonPie?" they asked the leader of the research teams. The team leader then gave this explanation.

It all started back in 1917, in the little Southern town of Chattanooga, Tennessee. In that fateful year, a traveling salesman told the Chattanooga Bakery how to make a MoonPie. It was incredibly simple: just put some marshmallow filling between two or three big, round graham-cracker cookies and cover them with chocolate coating. The result was a delicious snack. Today, millions of cultured and refined persons throughout America enjoy the creation of this genius.

The Japanese also discovered that the development of America as a powerful nation did not really begin until after 1917, the year the MoonPie was created. As millions of workmen eagerly looked forward to coffee-break time each morning and afternoon, they worked harder and faster as "MoonPie" time approached. This extra spurt of productivity made a tremendous contribution to American industry, which until now has not been officially recognized.

During World War II, the Chattanooga Bakery supplied millions of MoonPies to the defense plants of America. The production of guns, ships, tanks, trucks, and other military equipment far exceeded the wildest expectations of American military experts and helped them to win the war.

At this point, I would like to add that the explanation is very simple, of course, to knowledgeable MoonPie historians. Each day, unmarked trucks delivered allotments of the noble snack to the defense plants nationwide. The workers who met or exceeded production goals got MoonPies at break time.

As they leisurely munched on the noble snack, they relaxed, felt more content, and developed a strong feeling of team spirit and patriotism. When they finished their break, they could work harder and faster while keeping up the quality of their products. Some of you old-timers may remember that

Rosie the Riveter was frequently pictured with a half-eaten MoonPie by her side.

After the team leader finished his report, the Japanese leaders sat in silence for several minutes. Then, with a single brilliant insight, the captains of Japanese industry saw how to change their former image in a very simple way.

Of all the hundreds of nations in the world, they alone arranged a license agreement with the Chattanooga Bakery to make MoonPies in Japan. It was no accident that the Tohato Baking Company was located near the Japanese automobile plants. This little bakery also used unmarked trucks to deliver millions of Massi Pies, as they call the MoonPie, to the Honda, Toyota, Nissan, and other plants. Workers who met production and quality standards got MoonPies and tea at break time. The others got only dry rice cake. Much to the surprise of American and European industry, the Japanese cars quickly became famous for their clever designs, high quality, and long life.

Meanwhile in America, the captains of our automobile industry, located in lands of ice and snow, turned up their noses at the humble Southern snack and forced their workers to nibble on cheap junk food. You all know the sorry record of the American car industry, which produced lousy cars for many years.

A few years ago the Japanese Nissan Company announced that it would set up a plant in this country. Politicians in the lands of ice and snow eagerly sought the plant, but devoted fans of the MoonPie knew that it would be located close to the home of the MoonPie. Nissans are now assembled in Smyrna, Tennessee, just a fast two-hour drive up Interstate 24 from the Bakery.

Throughout this plant, in each vending area, there is a machine that sells only MoonPies in all thirty slots.

In December of 1985, the Toyota Motor Company announced that it would set up a plant near Lexington, Kentucky, about a four-hour drive up Interstate 75 from the Bakery. Honda cars are being made in Marysville, Ohio, just a little farther up I-75 from the Bakery. As the manager of one plant said, "Nothing must interfere with the delivery of MoonPies, for our entire plant would shut down without them."

In a spirit of patriotism, the Bakery started sending forty shipments a month to the auto plants in the Detroit area. An occasional hijacking of a load of MoonPies has quickly involved the FBI, customs agents, the State Department, army, and navy. They understand the importance of the noble snack in keeping America strong. A few months ago, John Kosik, executive vice president and general manager of the Bakery, was gone for over a week on a mysterious mission. Later he revealed he was helping the government track down a group of hijackers.

In another incident, you may remember the Walker family of spies. They were first caught at the Bakery, after years of spying, trying to steal the secrets of the Moon Pie for a foreign government. Before the Bakery's guards would turn them over to the FBI, however, the FBI had to promise not to mention the Walkers' attempts to infiltrate the Bakery. The Bakery, of course, did not want to attract any more spies.

The managers of the Chattanooga Bakery, in their great wisdom, have refused to hire scientists to explore the mysterious power of the MoonPie to inspire workers. No one completely understands how this humble snack creates feelings of contentment, joy, and humor. At the Bakery, they know they have a good thing. Their motto is "If it ain't broke, don't fix it." They offered this advice to the Coca-Cola Company, but it was ignored. You all know what happened to "New Coke." I need say no more.

Now you know the secret behind the invasion of quality cars from Japan.

The name of the MoonPie points to the sky. Some people see this as a challenge to man to learn to fly to the heavens in an effort to get closer to the source of the inspiration of our noble snack.

We all know, however, that *man will never fly*. That's for the birds. Men were put here to eat MoonPies and to drink.

We can only speculate on the fate of Wilbur and Orville Wright if they had been able to gain inspiration from the MoonPie. They might have been able to perfect their design of a car and keep it on the ground where it belonged.

Unfortunately, they started some fifteen years before the creation of the MoonPie. If they had only waited, we all might be driving "Wright-mobiles."

It is now my pleasure to introduce the lovely and charming Debbie Brown, who will teach you the etiquette and manners for savoring the delights of this delicious snack. By following her example, you will be able to properly enjoy the noble snack with other cultured and refined people at any time, at any place.

Talks to Civic Clubs

This is the basic version of many talks given to civic clubs, schools, nursing homes, churches, etc., since publication of the *Handbook* in 1985.

Often people are too stuffy and uptight in their work. As a result, morale and results often suffer. Some people have found that taking a humorous approach can produce surprising results and make more fun for everyone. Recently some professional researchers announced their discovery that humor on the job improved performance and morale.

It is my belief that intelligent people who are highly skilled in their jobs often have the best sense of humor. They use humor and courtesy to encourage a team spirit and to make working more fun. On the other hand, those who are just barely competent seem to have no sense of humor and often rely on the tactics of a dictator and a bully to manage their business.

Several years ago I worked for a large computer company in a division that wrote computer programs for hospitals. We had received some managers from lands of ice and snow who evidently copied their management style from Nazi storm troopers. Their heavy-handed approach and threatening attitude sent morale on a fast downhill slide.

Some of us felt that we needed to get some humor into the office to make it a pleasant place in which to work. We set up these rules:

> Humor must not rely on foul language.
> Humor must not make fun of any sex, race, religion, or political beliefs.
> Humor must be in good taste at all times in mixed groups.

Notice that we did not rule out making fun of pompous managers and stuffed-shirt supervisors. They seem to be everywhere. Some of you might have one or two in mind right now.

A few of my friends felt that these rules made it impossible to create humor. They dropped out of the group. Others took it as a great intellectual challenge and devoted themselves to this noble project with enthusiasm and intense dedication.

We thought that a running gag or joke would be a good starting place for this campaign. It had to be something simple and something identified with the South. After two days of research, we picked the two things that helped to make the South a great part of America: the MoonPie and an RC Cola. Needless to say, our managers from distant states did not understand what we were doing and left us alone. We seemed to be so harmless.

Instead of lasting just a few months, this project has continued for a dozen years and has reached across America and to Norway, Scotland, Australia, and New Zealand. It is amazing how a little humor can improve the quality of life on the job. The folks at the computer company later said that it was the best place at which they had ever worked. This was due largely to the fun and humor we added to the office.

Intelligent, creative people, like you, can find humor in simple things, as you will be seeing soon. It is my hope that each of you will try to find more humor in your daily life.

Concentrate on finding humor in the simple things in life. Develop your own style and see what happens. You may be pleasantly surprised.

Now let's enjoy a slide show that explains how the MoonPie Cultural Club is bringing culture and humor to the world. This is a spoof or takeoff on Masterpiece Theatre on public television. Perhaps a few of you have seen this program.

(The slide show lasts about twenty minutes. It is narrated by a distinguished radio announcer, Ellie Perzel, of Charlotte, North Carolina.)